Directory
of Eco-villages
in Europe

Hocamköy, Turkey

Directory of Eco-villages in Europe

Barbro Grindheim and Declan Kennedy
(editors)
Agnieszka Komoch
(lay-out)

Global
Eco-village
Network – Europe

ISBN 3-9802184-3-0

Published by
Global Eco-village Network (GEN)- Europe
Ginsterweg 5
31595 Steyerberg
Germany

Printed on Envirotop (100% recycled paper, 90g, matt) by
Weserdruckerei Rolf Oesselmann GmbH, Stolzenau, Germany

Price

1	Copy	Euro 15,-	DM 30,-
10	Copies or more	Euro 12,-	DM 24,- each
100	Copies or more	Euro 10,-	DM 20,- each

To order directly in Europe, please add Euro 3,- (DM 6,-) for packing and postage for the first book and Euro 1,- (DM 2,-) to the price of each additional copy. Send Eurocheque or money order (in Euro or DMs) or pay by VISA, mentioning your card number and its expiry date. For 100 copies or more, or for ordering from outside Europe, check shipping prices by calling GEN-Europe: +49 57 64 9 30 40 from 10 until 13 hrs GM time, or faxing +49 57 64 9 30 42.

Dyssekilde, Denmark

Gyürüfü, Hungary

Table of Contents

Table of Contents

Table of Contents

Terre d'Enneille, Belgium

Introduction

The work of compiling and editing the content of this Directory has been a fantastic journey from faraway corners of Russia, through the North of Norway to the Anatolian planes of Turkey. Most of the Eco-villages have written their own tales and stories and every one has the flavour of the respective language and their people. We thank them all for their co-operation. It is a generous encounter with people's dreams and visions, deep ecology and spirituality, manifesting into something very concrete: the creation of eco-villages.

It is also a practical handbook with a lot of ideas and inspiration for the ones who want to start and the ones who want to develop further. And, of course, the very intent of the Directory, making the connection between the ones who look for an Eco-village to visit, to learn from or to live in, and the eco-villages running teaching centres, needing the help of volunteers or those that are open to new members.

We have divided the eco-villages into two categories:
- *Existing Eco-village* and
- *Eco-village Initiative*

The *Existing Eco-villages* are well-established settlements with a lot of experience in decision-making, problem-solving and self-government. Most of them are rural or on the periphery of towns, a few are urban. The *Eco-village Initiatives* are in the starting phase. They all have acquired land and are designing and building their village or restoring already existing ones.

After the descriptions and contact addresses of eco-villages, we have included the addresses of the *Eco-village Networks and Nodes* in each country and of *Resource Centres* which provide information about and demonstration of alternative technologies.

It has been a great joy to receive descriptions and photos, to see what is happening in Europe and watching the Directory taking shape before our eyes. We have been in touch with about 200 people. In some cases, it was hard to make the decision whether this was an ecological project or an eco-village. If you feel that you qualify as an eco-village, we suggest that your group completes our Eco-village Profile assessment sheet, which is shown on page 183.

Since the work of this Directory is an on-going process, it will be updated as new information comes in, every two years. For this reason, we ask you to send descriptions and photographs of new (or to us unknown) eco-village projects to GEN-Europe by December 1999 for inclusion in the next issue.

Thank you again for your wonderful contributions. We needed your help. So much is happening now - so fast - as we come closer to the new millenium...

Barbro Grindheim   Lebensgarten, Steyerberg, June 1998

Ces, Switzerland

What is an eco-village ?

The eco-village is a manifestation of a great intuitive energy that comes from the deep understanding of nature and knows that both we and nature are both in real danger, urging us to look deeply again into what we have so casually and comfortably cast aside as though it were nothing but an outworn boot.

"Already . . . . more and more people think they are alone and lonely. It is true that they are alone - as all men must be if they are to grow into themselves - but loneliness is unnecessary, because the world contains so many close neighbours, the closest often the furthest away." (Laurens van der Post)

The eco-village model can be applied across the spectrum of present human settlements. It can be applied equally to both urban and rural settings, to developed as well as developing countries, providing solutions for meeting human needs, protection of the environment and an enhanced quality of life for all.

An eco-village in Hungary is different from an eco-village in Denmark, Spain or the UK. How does then the common community component articulate itself? Certainly there is collectivisation, almost at every level of an eco-village, as we have experienced over the last 13 years in Lebensgarten Steyerberg, Germany. Why else would we call ourselves a village? We feel connected to each other, even if some of us come from the North, some in the South, East or West, from an island or up in the mountains. The great power of the singular idea that ecology is relevant, yes urgent in our times, subsumes to some communal way. On the one hand, we experience an ever greater discord in personal opinion, in individualisation of the self, in the difficulty of accepting other's opinions, proposals or short-comings. Each eco-village is an island and the recognition of what we share often is narrowed to sectarian allegations, for instance, by sensational press.

On the other hand the negative of individuality is widely expressed in so-called democratic society. You do not have to look far to see evidence of this. Political apathy, social isolation, alienation, cultural deterioration, educational one-sided-ness have distorted and wounded the

Lebensgarten, Steyerberg

vitality of the individual spirit. Eco-village life can be a very potent antidote to this phenomenon, calling on the creative undertaking and the tolerance of the individual in a direct and stimulating way. In working with this model for development, we have worked with preserving the sense of place and community that already exists, while transforming our physical structures to reflect these deeper values.

The ideas that come up in all the eco-villages that are described in this book point towards therapy and healing in the broadest sense. The Global Eco-village Network (GEN) has been recognised for its work even though the eco-villages are still in the development stage. Some projects - still only barely an initiative - have been written about in the media, professional journals, have been praised by UN agencies and various dignitaries for their achievements. But there is not one class of healers and another to be healed. Evermore we all participate and suffer the inadequacies and deprivation of our modern urban and suburban settlements.

There is a fundamental tenet to the social-therapeutic work of the eco-village movement. The surrender of fixed ideas - of how one should live - has become a new experience borne out of a few decades of social discovery, therapeutic discovery, discovery of community and of the human. Such an orientation is attributed to the recognition of the eternal in each one of us and, in this way, when stated or not by one or other of the eco-villagers, the movement is intrinsically spiritual. We find ourselves in new landscapes: no longer in a tightly dictated village atmosphere, but in settings of challenge, discovery, growth - territories in which people are important and where the typologies and classifications are transformed or loose their traditional meaning.

What is the difference between a sustainable or intentional community and an eco-village ?

There are always considerable discussions about definitions and eco-villages are no exception. GEN has a discussion list on the Internet, called Eco Balance. We have discussions going on in article form between interested people, a draft has been put together by Hildur Jackson in Jan. 1998, including the Eco-village Profile. GEN has also an Eco-village Self-Audit whereby groups (who think they are such) can get a copy and go through the questionnaire to assess themselves - it is like a check list. All these documents can be sent out to you on e-mail (web and e-mail addresses below) or, if you have no access to the Internet, we can post you them as a print-out (we need Euro 3,- each to cover costs of copying and postage).

There has a lot been written and discussed about *sustainable communities* over the last decade or more, both in UN circles and at the local level. A sustainable community can be implemented by two or more persons on a farm, in a village or town, by a city, a region or a state. An eco-village is a sustainable community, but not all sustainable communities are eco-villages.

An *intentional community* is "basically any groups of two or more adults that choose to call itself a community". An eco-village can be and usually is a intentional community, but there are many intentional communities that have little or nothing to do with ecology and would not call themselves a village nor an eco-village.

Co-housing is a style of co-operative living that originated in Denmark, combining the autonomy of private dwellings with many of the resource advantages of community living. Usually initial residents participate in the planning and design of the community so that it directly responds to their needs. They can, but must not necessarily, be ecologically oriented. Often if they expand, they will consider themselves then as an eco-village.

A *village* is defined, on the Ekistic Scale by C. A. Doxiades and the World Society of Ekistics in the 1960's, as having 40 to 1500 inhabitants. It might have one or more neighbourhoods in it, but definitely has at least one shop or similar food outlet, some production of foods and goods for its own use and for export outside its boundaries. These factors vary from country to country and within countries from local culture to local culture. Very broadly defined, it is the entity between an hamlet and a town, and, usually, has its own local decision-making council or steering committee.

An *eco-village* is an intentional, sustainable community either in a rural, urban or sub-urban area. It has a membership and a decision-making body. It has no definite size - but will usually range in population from 50 to 3000 persons (these were the figures mentioned at the Findhorn Eco-village and Sustainable Community Conference 1995). It has all the aspects of a intentional community, a village or co-housing, as stated above, and an holistic ecological project in its aims, even if it has not reach the ultimate as yet. And it has more.

Almost all the eco-villages believe that by serving others we are serving ourselves - on a path towards greater self-knowledge and self-fulfilment. Everyone who visits an eco-village marvel at the atmosphere and the social cohesion. Pretty quickly, they can find their own place, their own way to take part in its work - for a shorter or longer period of time. It may be with special expertise or with information, it may be to mediate or just to understand or just to come and give love.

Everyone living in our human society who acquires any level of power feels a need to put it to good use, to change the world around them for the better. Giving support to an ecological project while living in it reflects this desire. It is not just giving a penny to a starving beggar, but you are participating in an effort to build an ecological settlement, to build a viable community - an eco-village - and, thereby, build a stronger base for a better and peaceful society.

Declan Kennedy
e-mail: declan@gaia.org
Self Audit: http://www.gaia.org/thegen/evaudit
Eco-balance: http://www.gaia.org/ecobalance

Ökosiedlung-Gärtnerhof

Austria
Gänsendorf
existing
eco-village

Ökosiedlung-Gärtnerhof is situated some 30 km Northeast of Vienna, within the city limits of Gänserndorf in the "Marchfeld" district, a region characterised by intensive farming and widely scattered weekend homes. Between 1982 and 1988 the future dwellers of the Eco-homes spent 4 years planning (under the guidance of the architect Helmut Deubner) and 2 years building a housing complex. It consists of 11 courtyard houses built as compact low rises with individual gardens, and 10 flats with terraces and roof gardens. The complex also includes a community room, a playground, landscaped public grounds, a swimming pond, vegetable gardens and an organic sewage treatment system. An adjacent nursery, the Gärtnerhof, has been operating bio-organically since 1978.

The most important goal during the planning period was to combine the natural interdependencies of energy, land, air and water, thereby creating an integrated system - departing from conventional systems of consumption and waste disposal.

Following aspects helped us to reach the desired objective:
- optimal use of simple, durable, and recyclable construction materials free of toxic substances
- an organic sewage treatment system
- passive and active utilisation of solar energy

15

Austria
Gänsendorf
existing
eco-village

Ökosiedlung-Gärtnerhof

- optimal insulation
- environmentally friendly, efficient heating
- using rainwater for washing machines, flushing toilets, watering plants and gardens, and, optionally, for personal hygiene
- individual garden plots
- composting toilets

The future dwellers strove to find a balanced ratio of inhabitants according to age, occupation and social strata. As far as planning allowed, there are differing sizes of residence, enabling both families and single persons to live in the complex. The complex is managed and maintained by the residents.

At present, there are about 100 inhabitants of the eco-homes more than 40 of them children. Originally, it was expected that many of the inhabitants would find employment within the project. So far only the project's architect, whose studio is located within the confines of the community, employs four or five residents. The Gärtnerhof nursery, which has lain idle for two years, is now being reactivated as a source

Ökosiedlung-Gärtnerhof

Austria
Gänsendorf
existing
eco-village

of productive activity for the physically and mentally handicapped. If, as anticipated, additional units are added to the Eco-homes community, this could also offer potential for more employment.

Regularly scheduled activities, often open to the public, take place in the community rooms. (Unfortunately the eco-homes community does not presently provide facilities for overnight accommodations.) Among others there have been courses on healing with Bach flowers remedies, gatherings of women's groups, dances, and initiation into the American Indian ritual of sharing the warmth of heated stones.

Contact:
Ökosiedlung-Gärtnerhof
Peter Lassnig
Hochwaldstrasse 37/7
2230 Gänsendorf
Austria

Tel: +43 14 84 73 10

Belgium
Durbuy
existing
eco-village

Terre d'Enneille

Terre d'Enneille is a shared community settlement welcoming friends of nature. It is an eco-spiritual village without creed or collective doctrine and organised as a coop. We do not represent a new religion or cult. We see ourselves as a meeting and experiential place gathering people with different spiritual paths or practices. We believe that when we align ourselves to our charter's values, and when we "exchange", we are able to create a lifestyle that respect the individual, the collective and the environment. Each of us consider ourselves as self-reliable and responsible for a part of planet - to manage it as ecologically as possible, to preserve nature and its diversity.

The eco-village is a place of sharing and exchange, where people wanting to base their life on Love and Peace come together. Love of all beings and of Nature, linked to the Consciousness, includes a planetary and ecological consciousness and responsibility. Through that Love comes the qualities of welcoming, respect, empowerment, personal transformation, non-judgement, discernment, realignment, honesty and forgiveness. These qualities will manifest themselves in co-operative behaviours, co-creation, mutual help, willingness to find the well-being of the whole as well as of the individuals, using consensus, inner-listening and atunement to take decisions; wanting to see beauty in ourselves, in others and all around, with joy and gratitude. All of this as an expression and incarnation of a spirituality anchored in the daily life.

- Consensus: a decision is made when every member can support it for the good of the whole, even if all of them would not have chosen it personally
- Inner-listening: to be open, beyond the emotional and the mental, to a Wisdom that is above our ego.
- Atunement : from a state of centring and alignment, to open ourselves and seek for Unity with others and the environment. It is often used at the beginning of an activity, when a decision is to be taken, or when a distortion needs to be lifted.

Terre d'Enneille is under construction since April 1992 and situated 12km from Marche-en Famenne, 7 km from Durbuy, 500 m from the river Ourthe and the small village of Grande-Enneille, 1h 30min from Brus-

18

Terre d'Enneille

Belgium
Durbuy

existing
eco-village

sels and Luxembourg. The place has 1ha of building ground for 12 houses, 1ha of land for the communal vegetable garden, orchard, worm farm and an ecological sewage system with reedbeds. The 4ha left are kept untouched for wild nature and managed as a nature reserve. This nature space is very rich and varied: wood, bushes, wet and dry meadows hosting a lot of wildlife. In the valley the spring becomes a little stream in which we have created a large pond. That is attracting a lot of species, some of them being endangered. We love this land and are willing to give it our care.

On a juridical base we are a coop. Therefore we are not owners, neither of the land nor of the houses, we have chosen to be custodians. The members abide by the charter. Each of us has taken shares in the coop. It gives individuals the right of occupancy of the house and the garden around, and the collective responsibility to care for the other 5ha. With

19

**Belgium
Durbuy**
existing
eco-village

Terre d'Enneille

this structure the land will be kept whole and out of any speculation. So far we have erected 6 houses, one being a 10 bed guest house. We are 10 full-time inhabitants, 3 buildings being dwellings. The houses are build on the basis of a "social standard" to enable everyone to join. Each person has is own source of income and life style. Some have bought the "village shares" for the house there are in, others have a renting-buying contract. Some people simply want to support the project and take "earth shares" to be part of the nature reserve protection. Others want to support people and take „support shares" that enable us to build. A low interest is given on the amount that is repaid within 10 or 15 years (+/- 5%). So far more than 90 people are part of the coop.

The village and the nature reserve is open to visitors every 4th Sunday afternoon and every Thursday at noontime. Please, phone before coming.

Contact:
Terre d'Eneille
Grande-Enneille 102 B
6940 Durbuy
Belgium

Tel/Fax.   +32 86 32 34 56
e-mail: terreen@ecovillage.org
web site: www.ecovillages.org/belgium/enneille

Village Convivial de la Paix-Dieux

Inspired by the Eco-village Conference at Findhorn in 1995 (and with more than two years of work) the association „Village convivial de la Paix-Dieu" was created in October 1997. Its aim is to circulate information about the concept of eco-villages in French and to promote the project of a convivial village. The site is situated at the end of the village of Jehay in the locality Dieu le Garde and blends in with the already existing village of Jehay.

Jehay is a small rural village situated between Liège and Namur, 4 km from a motor way exit. Nearby is the small town of Amay, a former town of brick makers with a rich artistic, cultural and artisan past which we would like to revive. Not far away you find the nuclear power station of Tihange (France) and the Tibetan Institute Yeunten Ling, well known world-wide.

The village is airy, situated in a green valley at the bottom of which flows the brook Paix-Dieu. It stretches between the castle of Jehay, a very distinctive monument of the Province of Liège, surrounded by a moat and woods, and the Abbey of Paix-Dieu, i.e. buildings of a former abbey of the Cistercian order dating back to the 12th century.
There is a magnificent project of restoration of the Walloon Region going on: to transform this abbey into a centre of training for ancient techniques, calling on the knowledge of craftsmen from different parts of Europe, and a school for craft apprentices.

The site of Dieu le Garde is a sloping plot of land of 12 ha between the village and the abbey. It is in these energies of peace, beauty and art that we have conceived a plan for an eco-village, consisting of about 75 housing spaces, a small nature reserve with a pond, a playground for children and teenagers, shops and a cultural centre. The plan was designed according to permacultural principles with collecting tanks and water purification tanks, various types of grouped or other housing, the possibility of building straw bale houses, waste management and dry toilets.

Respectful of the past, we want to restore a former pilgrimage path which ran across the village, defining the main axis of our village. The

Village Convivial de la Paix-Dieux

other local axes start from this one like the branches of a tree. They are narrower and follow the contour lines, creating protected spaces for walking, meeting people and playing in security.

At one end of the village we are planning a number of businesses with a social purpose oriented towards quality food, water management, information technology, telework, editing, multimedia production and artistic technology for light and sound.

At present one house has been built at one of the entries to the village, on the pilgrimage path, with certain ecological standards which were integrated.

Local government is very interested in our project and we are presently going through all the administrative steps for the acceptance of our plan.

The charitable association consists (at the moment) of about 11 members interested in living here. We meet once a month to create the glue of this basic group that will develop the village. New members are invited to present a written statement of their motivation to the administrative council, to pay their membership fee and to participate in the monthly meetings for six months in order to check whether they are in harmony with the basic vision. We know that the next step consists of creating activities within the basic group and start the building as soon as we have got the final government approval in the course of 1998.

Village Convivial de la Paix-Dieux

Belgium
Jehay
eco-village
initiative

Contact:
Village Convivial de la Paix-Dieux
Rue Gustave Robert 15
4540 Jehay
Belgium

Tel: +32 85 31 44 55
Fax: +32 85 31 16 37
e-mail: ecovillage@sia.be
website: www.ecovillages.org/belgium/paixdieux

Latinovac and the Farm Livadak

The village Latinovac is situated in the Golden Valley of Slavonska Pozega, 80 from Osijek. The railway connects the village with the town of Slavonska Pozega (30 klm) via Nosice and there is a bus line to the village Caglin which is 2 kilometres away. Latinovac lies at an altitude of 97 metres in the valley of pure nature surrounded by the Slavonian mountains. A mountain path leads to the Sovsko Lake, an ideal holiday resort.

The village houses are built of mud or fire-baked bricks. Many of them are ramshackle buildings. The village has electricity. In every house potable water is obtained from 12 meter deep wells. Water is of excellent quality and taste.

120 inhabitants live in the village. Most of them are Serbs but there are also Croats and Hungarians. During the war in 1991/92 several displaced families from Vukovar settled in the village. Most of the inhabitants are elderly people. The young ones left because of bad economic situation. The remaining children attend the primary school in Caglin because both the primary school and the community centre have been closed. Nevertheless, these buildings have partly been restored, but are still in need of repair. Latinovac and its inhabitants have preserved their identity and loyalty to their region and the Croatian state during the war of 1991/92. The newcomers have successfully integrated. We think it is very important to sustain such atmosphere and develop it further so that we can learn from this example.

The eco-village group are using these premises for the following activities:
- cultural events (films, concerts, dances, theatre performances)
- gathering of women groups for embroidery and ceramics
- gathering of inhabitants for traditional festivities, dances and customs
- workshops for children (to stimulate creativity and calm stressful situations)
- seminars, lectures and workshops for the local inhabitants concerning ecology, health and permaculture
- weekend or one-day workshops on communication, conflict resolution, understanding and acceptance of differences, reactions to

Latinovac and the Farm Livadak

stressful situations, personal and spiritual development, forgiveness and reconciliation
* meetings and lectures on mountaineering as a way of improving quality of life and health

The eco-village group, founded in May 1995, are now 15-20 people and swell to more especially through volunteers in the summer. Four or five councellors are often coming from Lebensgarten Eco-village, Germany, who are also very practical in getting new sub-projects going. The basic aim of the eco-village project is to practise ecological, healthy, tolerant attitudes towards ourselves, other people and nature. This requires personal involvement and working on a communal level.

The eco-village project for Latinovac is a non-party, non-profit, non-governmental activity. The beneficiaries of the project are:
* local population (farmers, children, women, younger people)
* displaced persons (on returning home they could promote this experience)
* activists of psycho-social and health groups, people dealing with interpersonal and spiritual relations, eco groups, etc

Latinovac and the Farm Livadak

One of the project aims is also to preserve and revive cultural heritage, to learn from the tradition and life style of this place which has been composed, through centuries, of various ethnic groups. Latinovac is a place where communities could exchange experiences, show  mutual respect, work on trust, forgiveness and reconciliation. The immediate work includes:

- renewal of public buildings (primary school, the community centre)
- repairing the houses owned by the members of the eco-village project so that guests, lecturers and participants can be accommodated during workshops
- buying land that would be cultivated according to the principles of permaculture
- buying one minibus for the transportation of guests
- fund-raising for covering the costs of lectures, workshops and seminars

Contact: Branka Drabek-Milekic
The Farm Livadak
Latinovac 11
34380 Caglin
Croatia
Tel: +385 34 22 15 83

or
Reljkoviceva 16
31000 Osijec
Croatia
Tel: +385 314 50 53
e-mail: ekoselo-latinovac@zamir-zg.ztn.apc.org

The ideas for the first Danish eco-village were formulated in 1982.
1988: The Eco-Village (EV) buys the farm Dyssekildegård, incl. 13 ha of land, 5 ha of which is housing zone. An untraditional and flexible district plan is designed with 5 co-housing groups to finance the project.

1990: Only 25 members out of 110 are ready to finance the project. The budget must be reduced to about 15% in order to get started. At last 65 members of EV continue with the plan.

1991: The first 14 houses are built.

1992: Parents have started a private kindergarten on the farm. Later it receives municipal support and moves to „Villaro", next to the farm. The first section of 6 apartments for leaseholders is built.

1994: The second section of 8 apartments is ready.

1997: There are now about 60 adults and 25 children living in EV. A broad spectrum of ages, trades and social status is represented. About half the building lots have been sold. Membership is open!

From ideas to practical ecology: caring for human beings, animals, plants and environment was defined as the superior common goal - an

Dyssekilde

expression of a global ecological out-look. The wish to realise whole-ness in our fragmented lifestyle by integrating housing, self-suffi-ciency and local trades has been foremost in creating the foundations of the common vision. In practice we try to combine architecture, re-newable energy, water treatment, agriculture and trades. Furthermore we would like to create a spiritual community and set up new social activities.

Each member pays to EV a deposit which is at present 8.900 Dkr and an additional 3.000 Dkr per year to cover overall expenses. Building lots cost 1.000 Dkr per m² of the gross area of the house. All members have a direct influence on the development and growth of the commu-nity through quarterly meetings. Here, more long term decisions are made, whereas the daily running is managed by working groups and the steering committee.

The housing zone is divided into 5 different groups of co-housing struc-ture and facilities which have their own individual character and mana-ge their own areas. We try to avoid private fences and hedges. Cars are parked only at the parking lot.

The Dome Group: The practical reason for choosing the dome shape is that materials and heat loss is reduced by about 30% (even more in extreme conditions). Aesthetically it feels closer to nature. Prices are 7-10.000 Dkr/m². The domes are the first prototypes of their kind in Denmark.

Dysager: An experimental housing group was started in 1987. Owner builder houses, several have made their own designs and used recycled materials: Bricks, tile, timber, glass, boards and even straw and paper insulation, all houses are approved by the Danish building codes, at 5-8.000 Dkr/m²

Solpletten: The southern row of this group consists of 3 passive-solar houses. They have underfloor heat storage and insulated windows. New houses in the northern row can be individual, two twin-houses, at 6-8.000 Dkr/m²

Højager: So far 14 rowhouses for lease-holders have been built by our own crew. Another 8 apartments and a common house are planned. Passive solar design, extra insulation (also insulated windows), solar heated water and green-houses are standard, but the rent is still kept at a reasonable level.

The 5th Group: This group will be situated north of the dome group. We are interested in individual, low houses for rent or shares as well as a section consisting of inexpensive solutions for young people.

Next to the housing groups there are building lots for commercial purposes for rent or sale. Several inhabitants have created local jobs.

The Torup Village Centre is a co-operation between EV and the other inhabitants in Torup. The wings of the old farmhouse will gradually be rebuilt into a community centre with workshops, a meeting hall and rooms for other cultural activities. The first stage will be a meeting hall with kitchen, office etc.

Community and development: We expect new members to join in the decision-making of the community and in the different working groups like gardening, building, info-work, maintenance of the farm, waste separation, water treatment, etc. Common activities may require 3-4 hours a week per member. We also have evening activities with handicrafts, singing, music, meditation, etc. and we have many organised and spontaneous celebrations. Conflicts and the balance between common and individual interests are brought up for discussion continuously, when the need arises. It develops both the individual and the community.

Agriculture: We are self-sufficient with organic vegetables. The individual members can join the agriculture group and the community vegetable scheme or they can have a small private vegetable garden. We also have a small livestock of goats, sheep and hens.

Water Treatment: Our consumption of drinking water is 60-65% of the average. Recycled water and rain water is used for toilets and watering gardens. A Biological water treatment system has been built and ap-

Dyssekilde

proved in accordance with the Camphill design in England. Both grey and black water is organically treated, filtered vertically by gravity. 6 houses have compost toilets.

Resources: Recycling of resources takes place on a regional basis: Glass and bottles, paper, clothes, batteries, metal and certain plastics. Organic material is given to the animals (food waste) or composted.

Energy: In most of our house, active solar systems include various kinds of collectors for water heating or perhaps heat storage under the floor. Passive systems let heavy walls and floors absorb solar heat. Several houses have Finnish mass stoves made of 2-4 tons of bricks. In 1994, Halsnæs Windmill Co erected a 450 kW m windmill on our land.

Transport: From Dyssekilde station, next to EV, the local railway runs to Hundested and to Hillerød. The trip from Copenhagen to Torup lasts 80 min.

Guided tours: From May until October there are guided tours on Saturdays at 3 pm (in winter only in even weeks).The fee is 30 Dkr per adult and the tour takes 1-2 hours. Group tours (max 25) at other times are arranged at 600 Dkr. The office is open on weekdays from 10 am to 2 pm. Occasionally the cafe is open on Saturdays from 2 pm to 5 pm. Visitors may join the common vegetarian evening meals at a reasonable price. (Please call in advance during office hours.) A camp site, where visitors can stay one or two nights at 20 Dkr per adult, two big tipies, compost toilets, solar showers, fire places and a splendid view are available. Courses are held frequently in African drums, tai chi, yoga, dome building, agriculture, etc.

Contact:
Hågendrupvej 6, Torup
3390 Hundested
Denmark

Tel/Fax: +45 47 98 70 26
e-mail: moondome@centrum.dk

Hertha ECOmmunity is situated in Jutland, near Aarhus in the little village of Herskind. It consists of about 50 inhabitants + 13 developmentally retarded young people. The first people moved in in 1995. We have a goal of a sustainable settlement for about 200 people.

We have developed a main concept which we call reverse integration i.e. the „normal people" integrate with the handicapped instead of the

other way around. In this way the retarded young benefit from the normal life of people having their rhythm, and the „normal" benefit from the resources (the spontaneity, the heart and the openness) of the retarded, something often missing in a „normal" adult world.

The other main concept is that we believe that if this (and any) settlement is to be sustainable, it needs to build not only on „technical" ecology, but on a social ecology. Out of the „social" the „technical" ecology rises. Thus we work consciously on creating a humane society, which has often a reserve of strength. If this strength is used to „lift" a group of weak citizens, they will find themselves in a more equal life situation, beneficial and necessary for both the „weak" and the „strong". In this way the „normal" integrate with the handicapped.

We have a high degree of ecology in the buildings of the area and our 55 acres of agriculture are grown biodynamically. The workshops for

Hertha

the young retarded consist of weaving, bakery, gardening and farming and more is to come..

1995-98, seven houses were built and at present (April ´98) three more are under construction and plans are made for 5 flats for rent. All of the buildings are designed, following some of the architectural impulses of Rudolf Steiner. Anthroposophy is likewise the main impulse in decision making, treatment of the handicapped, etc. - however, in a very non-dogmatic way.

Finally, it should be mentioned that we have won lots of prizes. In 1997, we won a second prize of 150.000 Dkr. for an essay on „Sustainable Settlements in the 21th. century", which had been organised by Gaia Trust and the Danish Association of Sustainable Communities in co-operation with 5 Danish government departments. This makes us very proud. We also experience great support from national and international foundations and banks.

Our goal for the forthcoming few years is that we get even more activities going within the community as a whole. A start would be a kind of

village hall with a café with a little shop, some offices, computers, together with the existing bakery. Among other things, this would make it possibly for us to take better care of the many visitors that ask for information. So we continue making lots of plans.

Contact:
Allan Elm
F/ Hertha Levefællesskab
Landsbyvænget 14, Herskind
8464 Galten
Denmark

e-mail: allanelm@hotmail.com

Hjortshøj

Andelssamfundet in Hjortshøj (The Co-operative Society in Hjorts-høj), a social/ecological community, is located 15 km north of Aarhus. We are currently two housing groups with 78 people. Our goal is a self-sufficient eco-village of 500 people. Visions of this co-operative society were formed in 1986. Our first house was built in 1991, but as a community with working groups, vegetable gardens, communal meals and celebrations, we only exist since 1996. We have succeeded in making a practical example in the right direction of a self-sufficient lifestyle. Seen in light of the time we now live in, it is something we can be proud of. And we are!!!

In many ways we live a very „normal" life contradictory to the prejudices surrounding us. We too use computers, cars and machines for agricultural purposes. Our aim is not to live in a closed society, but to create a lifestyle where we combine new technological knowledge with sustainable values in a setting where many people can imagine themselves living.

Since we know there are many ways to make these first steps, we will never claim that we have found the definitive answers. We will, how-

ever, tell you why we think it is a good idea to use compost toilets and unburned clay bricks.

Group 1: 10 private houses, the last house was finished in 1996, with 28 people including 11 children. The people who live in these houses were involved in the whole building process, which included drawing and building the houses as well as designing the interior.

Group 2: 20 residences and a community house. These houses for 50 people, including 25 children, were finished in 1996 and are owned by  a Building Society. In co-operation with the architects and the Building Society, the residents also had influence on the interior design. It is the first time that a Building Society was involved in building ecologically sustainable houses. This is particularly important for people who wish to live in this form of housing, yet do not want to or cannot afford to build their own house.

Group 3: this group will include 11 private houses and a community house, soon to be built for 26 people, including 9 children. The group will continue the experience already gained in the community and will improve grey water treatment through evaporation and by using a grove of willow trees for nutrient retention and evaporation of excess water.

Group 4: This group is in the making and are looking for a Building Society to help finance and build their houses.

Building concepts include:
• locally extracted materials as far as possible
• houses with breathable materials, walls of unburned clay, wood, plaster, and recycled paper as isolation

Hjortshøj

- houses with wood siding of red cedar or spruce treated with oil paint
- paints, mixed according to old recipés, based on water, oil, raw materials and colour pigments

Resources:
- sustainable energy such as passive and active solar energy
- water conservation such as collecting rainwater for washing clothes, using compost toilets and water conserving installations
- creating local product circulation as far as possible by recycling, composting and treating grey waste water on the site
- a critical view as a consumer

Social life and work:
- social life often arises from the work we do together
- all work concerning the community is voluntary
- there is a wish to create jobs within the community
- celebrations fill in the need of being together outside work situations
- there is the possibility to eat in the community house 3 days a week

Work, meetings and celebrations have helped us to get to know each other well and give a close daily contact. It is different how much each person takes part in the work and socialising. However, we live here because we want to make something of this place and practically this means that people do what they are good at.

For guests who would like to stay for one or more days there is a possibility to stay overnight in the community house, a good way of getting a look into our daily life is by participating on working days. Otherwise, every second Sunday (odd weeks) at 2 p.m. there is a guided tour, lead by one of the residents. For larger groups contact: Peter Myatt (phone: 45-86227484)

Contact:
Ulla Trædmark Jensen
Hjortshøj Møllevej 188
8530 Hjortshøj
Denmark

Tel: +45 86 74 21 88
web site: http://www.gaia.org/los/hjortshoj/index.html

Svanholm

One hundred Danish people collectively purchased a large farm property in 1978; the Svanholm Estate which lays 60 kilometres Northwest of Copenhagen. We paid 30 million Dkr (i.e. £3 mill. pounds sterling or U$ 4.6 mill.) for 253 hectares (625 acres) of farmland and 195 hectares of woodlands, residences and park land, which contains luscious meadows and marshes.

We wanted an integrated lifestyle and a true community where we could decide for ourselves how we want to live and work together, a place where we and our children could thrive with animals, abundant nature and fresh air. Our intention was (and is) to develop rural production based on equally shared work, shared economy and shared decision-making. Now, we are indeed a thriving community, a living, growing organism. We have seen many changes and exciting developments along the way. Though we cannot (yet) finance all our dreams, there is no shortage of experimental plans and projects that we try out or want to undertake.

Organic farming is our main interest and work centre, one of a dozen job sites at our collective country home. We grow several kinds of grains for human consumption and animal feed, as well as vegetables and fruits. The crop of carrots, potatoes and onions is sold through Denmark's leading co-op supermarket chain and - in smaller amounts - at a shop on our own premises and at Lyngby Mølle near Copenhagen. We also produce and sell ecological milk from our 100 cows.

Overall visions, budgets and planning are set by all members. Our highest decision-making authority is the weekly communal meeting.

We do not vote, avoiding me-against-you syndromes, rather discuss our way to agreement on a consensus basis. We strive to implement ecological ideas based on sustainable development; we endeavour to create a holistic lifestyle, meeting people´s needs harmoniously without jeopardising future generations and nature as well.

We get a lot of enquiries from individuals, groups and institutions who want to know more about our life and ideas at Svanholm. (Unfortunately we don't have any positive experience with trying to get a staying and working permit for potential guest from non-European Union countries, so we had to give up. We're truly sorry.) We like to meet these requests as far as possible, both by showing visitors around, and by going out to give lectures. We also sell a booklet, „Self-Government at Svanholm". All enquiries should be in writing.

Contact:
Visitors Group
Svanholm Gods
Svanholm Allé 2
4050 Skibby
Denmark

web site: http://www.gaia.org/los/svanholm/index.html

Udgaarden

Udgaarden is located in the Danish village of Lading and is a lively and thriving community. It was started in July 1992. Udgaarden consists of 15 low energy houses, one communal house and a farm built around a courtyard. About 30 adults and 30 children live here in a co-operative housing association.

We do organic farming and have a mixture of animals on our 48 acres of land. Farming is done communally with the farming group taking the main responsibility, so there is plenty of opportunity for everybody

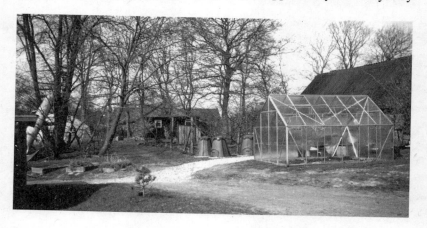

to work together. We also eat our organic produce together 5 evenings a week and sometimes come together to celebrate smaller and bigger events in everyday life.

Udgaarden does not follow a spiritual direction, nor does it have a political programme. It is most important for the residents of Udgaarden to be part of the local community and not a seperate, little island. We think we have accomplished this through our farming, our residents association, our child care facilities, our football club and generally through being good neighbours.

According to our articles of association, all residents need to buy a share when moving in and agree to the farm being run organically.

The 15 houses in the association are heated on a combination of solar panels and wooden chips, through a central heating installation. The blue wooden houses all face south and have extra insulation and double glazing. The heating bill for each house per month is very low, at present about 250 Dkr per month. We have a large rainwater storage system, designed to provide water for washing machines and toilets. We are working on some plans for a windmill to make us self-sufficient with electricity.

We are open to visits and tours of the site but it is necessary to call in advance to arrange your visit. It will cost a small amount depending on the size of the group.

Contact:
Udgaarden
Eric Olsen
Udgaarden 18
8471 Sabro
Denmark

Tel: +45 86 94 96 18
web site: www.gaia.org/los/udgaardenilading/index.html

Munkesoegaard

Munkesoegaard is an eco-village being build in Trekroner near Roskilde. It is just half an hour by train from the centre of Copenhagen. The goal is to establish a small community based on environmentally sustainable solutions, occupied by people from different backgrounds, education and economies. It is a place with the possibilities for greater social integration among the inhabitants.

The idea for the village was formed in 1995 when a small association was founded. The purpose was to investigate the possibilities and even-

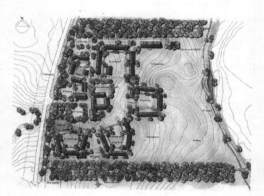

tually establish an eco-village. Much discussion and planning was done during the first year and, in the summer of 1996, we chose the site in Roskilde as the best site for the village. In the autumn of 1996, contacts with one of the co-operative housing societies in Roskilde was established, but it was not until the summer of 1997 that an agreement with the housing society was made. Different work groups have discussed and planned technical solutions for the village, and in the autumn of 1997 a group of architects and engineers was contacted to formalise these plans. Until then all work on the project had been done by the future occupants. Building will commence in the summer of 1998, with the first families moving in during the spring of 1999.

The village is divided into five groups each of 20 houses/apartments, placed around the common farmhouse. The five groups are of different forms of ownership and occupants. One is owner occupied houses, one is co-operatively owned. The last three groups are on rental basis; one group is for young people under the age of 31, one group is for seniors over the age of 50 and the last group is on ordinary rental basis. All in all a village with around 200 grown ups and 90 children of all ages.

Each group has its own common house where there will be common meals on a daily basis, place for children to play and place for long term guests. An area of 24 hectares around the village is for organic farming by the people from the village that might be interested in it.

The village is based on ecological principles with the least possible load on the environment. This is achieved through local circuits of Energy, water and waste, and by the choice of environmentally friendly building methods and materials. The architecture of the village is considered important: variety within a clear common character for the whole site has been adapted.

Each group consists of three two storey buildings in the shape of a horseshoe and with the common house on the fourth side. All homes have an entrance from the inside of the horse shoe, and a small terrace/ garden in connection with the house. Some of the dwellings are row houses, and others are apartments.

The load-bearing construction is wood, the outer walls and roof are highly insulated, the outer shell is made from wood and the roof is covered by reused tiles. The walls between the houses are made from

Munkesoegaard

rammed mud bricks made on the site. Other walls are covered by gypsum boards. Unheated weather porches, made from glass, will be built onto south facing facades.

The houses are heated by under-floor heating. The heat is supplied by a wood chip fired central heater combined with a Stirling motor for power generation. During the summer, warm water is supplied from solar panels on the common house roofs.

All houses have a compost toilet with urine separation. The compost is collected in a container in a small cellar, and the urine is flushed to a central tank. This toilet reduces the water consumption of water by 20%, reduces the outlet of problematic waste to the local stream, uses less energy and recycles nutrients to the land. The whole village is not connected to the city sewage system. The gray waste water from bath, kitchen and washing is treated locally in a system of sand filters and then led to the local stream. Rain water is collected from the roofs and used for washing of clothes.

The common houses are made with facilities for eating, with large kitchen, common laundry, and guest rooms. The size of the common houses is around 8 to 10% of the total housing area.

The whole village is planned by the same set of architects and engineers, and all major building activities will be made by professional construction companies. There is possibility for the owner of houses to do some of the interior by themselves. These strict rules are made to prevent some of the building to stand unfinished for longer periods of time.

Contact:
Lars Levin-Jensen
Bondehavevej 20, 1.th
2880 Bagsvaerd
Denmark

web site: http://www.gaia.org/losdanish/okobo (most of it is in Danish.)

An eco-village has naturally come into being in the village of Isnäs, on the Southern coast of Finland, 70 km East of Helsinki. A large (140 ha) biodynamic farm of Labby Manor has been operating in the village for the last ten years. Throughout the development of the farm there has

been the goal of forming a larger community around it and of implementing new social impulses. A great leap was taken in this direction in the spring of 1997 when a group of about ten people, involved with the farm, formed a co-operative named Aurinko & Okra (Sun & Ochre; the colour of earth).

The co-operative purchased four large buildings and 2,5 ha at the old Isnäs saw mill from a multi-sector corporation. The saw mill had been closed down in 1990. The property of the co-operative consists of three wooden buildings built in 1898 to house the saw mill workers and a slightly newer wooden building which has housed the offices as well as the supervisor's apartment. All buildings are under historic preservation. The final purchase of the property took place in March 1998. In order to make such a purchase, the co-op has to take a loan from a commercial bank and we are working to find more ethical sources of funding to replace this loan as soon as possible.

The co-op has chosen ecological tourism and ecological catering as its livelihood. Rooms are being repaired in the buildings for bed & break-

Aurinko & Okra

fast accommodation, a café was run in summer 1997 and was extended to serve lunches in spring 1998. A number of courses on ecological topics have been held. Aurinko & Okra has become well known for its delicious biodynamic food at many seminars where we have catered. We offer travellers guided nature and cultural tours by foot or horse, rent out bikes and boats - and do our best to bring life back to this village, so troubled by unemployment.

The co-op and Labby farm form an organic whole. Many of the members of the co-op (presently there are 14 members) and non-members who live in the co-op's houses work on the farm. The co-op caters lunch for the farm. The farm produces most of the ingredients the co-op needs for its café and catering business and is one of the main

attractions for the people visiting. Labby is best known for its wide variety of spice and tea herbs, but produces also grains, vegetables, meat, wool and small quantities of milk products. There is a farm shop selling home-grown products as well as a wide range of other ecological products. The farm includes a large area of natural meadows and wetlands - a vanishing cultural landscape and home to many species of rare plants and numerous species of birds. During the growing season there are often 20 people working on the farm, mostly volunteers and practicants. The winter 97-98 ten people were working on the farm which is more than in previous winters.

To advance the common goals of the farm, the co-op and other ecologically minded residents and friends of the area, a non-profit association named Culture and Landscape Association Saarni has been formed and registered. The association carries out biological, historical, geographical and cultural research in the area and organises courses. In July 1997, the association co-ordinated the first annual „Sahalla Soi!" music and arts festival at the saw mill. The festival will take place on the last weekend of July every year.

Besides these three groups, the handicrafts workers (boat building, felt work, candle and jewellery making) and the other ecological farmers of the village and the surrounding area add to the organic totality which can be described as a very fine ecological village indeed.

Finland

Aurinko & Okra

Each of the units makes their own decisions and, even within the co-op and the farm, smaller groups decide about practical matters pertaining to their work independently. Decision making is based on the ideal of consensus and voting is unusual, though included in the co-op's charter. Because the same people are involved in the co-op, the farm and the association, the flow of information is guaranteed.

We welcome visitors; A bed with breakfast at the saw mill costs 120-140 FIM, a tent site 40 FIM, a hostel style accommodation with a price somewhere between the above will become available later. The café and the farm shop are open on the weekends. Rooms can also be rented at 600 - 1000 FIM/ month, the rent may be paid as repairs on the room. We also welcome volunteer workers; please contact us well in advance and tell about yourself and your interests. The co-op accepts members, preferably members with a specific skill that is of use to the community. Membership fee of the co-op is 2000 FIM.

Isnäs village is located on the coast of the Gulf of Finland between the towns of Porvoo and Loviisa. Travelling by car; take the road 1571 East out of Porvoo until you reach Isnäs (about 25 km) where Aurinko & Okra signs will guide you. Busses from Porvoo arrive at the Isnäs bar (about 2 km from the saw mill); phone or ask directions at the bar. If you are travelling by boat, locate Isnäs on the sea chart and follow the 4 m deep channel to the saw mill.

To receive information about the progress of our work, the courses and cultural events and to simply make contact:

Labby Biodynamic Farm
Box 275 E
07750 Isnäs
Finland

Tel: +358 19 63 44 99
Fax: +358 19 63 46 01
e-mail: juha.nari@iuakk.fi

The first community, founded in Finland solely for ecological sustainability, started with ten people June 1997 in Ähtäri. We are not professional farmers but older people (40-60), wanting to live in the countryside away fom the 8-hours workday. We also have younger people searching for a life with little or no consumption.

The place is marvellous with clean lakes and an old forest around it, cattle meadows and gardens, an abandoned old peoples home with two separate wooden houses, a cowshed, 6 separate apartments, sauna and a chapel. The main building is typical of the 1950's: basement for acti-

vities, first floor for kitchen, dining room and large rooms, second floor for residence. There are 40 rooms and place enough for 35 people. We have 10 hectares of land and 700 meters of beach.

We aim at exploring and promoting ecological lifestyles, by minimising our use of products that involve animal, human or environmental exploitation, going towards self-sufficiency. We recycle most waste and are building compost toilets. We use wood for heating and warm water. We are developing our site as a living exhibition of sustainable land use and sustainable living practices. Organic gardening, animal care and estate management are using permaculture design techniques. We

Kaijamkoti

want to be an educational centre from which ecological and alternative lifestyle concepts would be brought to a wider audience. We are planning to set up a Permaculture Foundation with the object of buying the estate and educating the public in matters concerning the environment and conservation, ecologically sound food production and energy use, in other words: sustainable living.

We have furnished the rooms simply. We eat together and have one communal kitchen. Our food is basic Finnish food, we eat what is growing in this climate: potatoes, carrots, all kinds of onions, herbs, tomatoes, rutabagas and beetroots. We also eat fresh-water fish, chikken and the meat of local animals which are not killed in a slaughter-house. Two of us share the daily responsibility of looking after the animals. We have sheep, chickens, goats, cats and dogs. We have a space for two horses, two cows and two pigs. Workshops have included organic and biodynamic gardening, tantra and tao sexuality.

People normally visit for 2 to 3 days the first time. Working visitors are welcome. You pay 150 FMK for board and lodging and work for four hours in our house, garden or cowshed. Or making cheese, yoghurt and home made bread. You can also work with us in the nearby forest: coppicing, felling and clearing for firewood, picking berries and mushrooms.

The community members do not share income, but each one pays 1500 FMK per month for room and board. We discourage full time jobs outside. A number of people still work part-time outside teaching, writing, building consulting, etc. Many have pensions and some are on unemployment. Some people earn the living consulting for an ecological Russian project. There is no capital required to join. The age of members range at the moment from 1 year to 66. Individuals can have their own room or live as a couple. In addition to the communal kitchen, there is a sitting room, library, television room, laundry and two saunas.

Ähtäri is a popular tourist resort in the heart of Finland. There is the Wildlife Park, where one can meet the natural inhabitants of the northern forests. It is the home of some 300 wild animals of different ages, representing about 60 species (elk, bear, lynx, etc.). The native Nordic animals all live in natural environments and can be seen along a three-kilometre walk.

Chapel: meditation 7-7.20 and 21-21.20 hrs.
Smoke sauna: Tuesday and Saturday
Milking time: 8-9 and 19-20 hrs.
Eating times: 12 and 17 hrs. (breakfast, tea break and nightbite everyone takes themselves from the kitchen)
Saturday: cleaning and baking day

Contact:
Kaijamkoti
Suomineito-yhteisö
Kaijantie 283
63700 Ähtäri
Finland

Tel: +358 65 33 06 01
Fax: +358 65 33 53 23
Mobile: +358 50 584 92 86
e-mail: Marketta.Horn@helsinki.fi

Finland
Tampere
existing
eco-village

Kangasala

Our village project started in 1993. For a long time we searched but then found a suitable place for the project near Tampere. Finally Kangasala offered a plot with which the members felt comfortable and the project was ready to begin. In the meantime many of the original members had already found their own homes elsewhere. So today the assembly of the group is rather different than the original set-up.

The village consists of nine households - 17 adults and 16 children. The main building material will be wood. In the middle of the village there will be a district heating centre, which will use wood-chips. The building has been built to the roof phase, but has not the needed technical equipment yet. All the houses will have compost toilets. There will not be any municipal drain in the project, but the sewage will be handled locally. The used system is called „Green-Pack". The grey water will be filtered and will go through reed and rushes. In this way it is clean enough to be leached into the ground.

There is also a field in our village area, so that it is possible for people to grow food. Some members are also dreaming of having animals: hens, sheep, bees and horses. None of us are a real farmers, but everyone is interested. Let us see what happens. The majority of us have a technical background: engineers, architects and computer people, also a kindergarten teacher and a fireman.

Contact:
Kangasala Ekokyla
Siitamaentie 752
36120 Suinula
Finland

Tel: +358 405 03 62 22
e-mail: pia.s.niemela@nmp.nokia.com

Katajamäki (Juniper Hill) is an old nature sanatorium, functioning since the beginning of the century. At present, it is a small eco-commune and a course centre with cultural activities. We try to build up the place to be a permacultural forest garden-village. Katajamäki is situated in the middle of southern Finland, about 100 km east of Tampere and about 300 km north of Helsinki.

In winter of 1997/98, we were 7 adults and some children living in the place. In the summertime, the number of people doubled. In addition there is space for visitors and volunteers. We have domestic animals like a horses, goats, hens, dogs, cats and bees. In the close surrounding natural areas, there are also many wild animals (e.g. ravens, eagle, owls,

fox, bears, moose, etc.). Katajamäki is situated besides a protected old forest area: Life's Hill and Life's Lake - with still very clean water.

The property was rented for the last four years before it was bought in March 1998 by the newly formed Association of Katajamäki. The place is owned entirely by the Association which so far has about 15 members - taking part in the costs of the place monthly and each having rooms named after them.

Finland
Vilppula
existing
eco-village

Katajamäki

So far there is a main house and two other living houses with several other buildings, like storehouses, a roomy sauna house, and tipis, altogether about 25 rooms with different uses. There is also a special camping area by the lake. The amount of land is about three hectares on the hill and half of a hectare by the lakeside.

Our courses and cultural activities deal with handicraft (like drum making, felting, repairs), use of natural products, group processes, and environmental activism; often in connection with our own needs. Visitors have to pay about 8$ per day. We will organise a cultural festival together with our different friendship groups annually in August/September.

Our vision is to buy another 10 hectares of partly logged forestland in the surroundings for new buildings and forest gardens, within the next few years. By then, we hope to be about 15-20 adults living here throughout the year. The new settlements will be built using mostly natural materials and natural forms. Katajamäki is continuously in a building process and needs volunteers.

The place was used as a youth summer camp centre for nearly fifty years. This means that the project is fairly unspoiled by modern recon-

54

ditioning - and it has not been used in winter time for quite a long time. For heating the houses, we use woodfuel, which could be called *local sun energy*, that we gather free or buy from local farmers. There is a massive stove in every room, which means that there is no waste of energy.

We have small gardens for vegetables and herbs, not fields. The forest gives us lots of herbs, mushrooms, berries etc., and the lake gives us fish. We endeavour to buy or exchange the main part of our food from local farmers, many of them producing biological products.

Katajamäki has actively been connected in the Finnish Eco- Society Project having connections to about 45 different kinds of communities mainly in the countryside in Finland. We have also good connections to the Friends of the Earth in Finland.

Contact:
Kai Vaara
Katajamäki
35700 Vilppula
Finland

Tel: +358 34 71 80 40
e-mail: atkava@uta.fi

Keuruun Ekokylä

The Keuruu Eco-village is situated on a beautiful southern slope of the Kivijärvi lake in Middle Finland about 70 kilometres to the West from Jyväskylä. The community was founded in June 1997 and has now 20 inhabitants. There is space for more than 50 persons who want to live ecologically. It is moving towards functioning as a permacultural model.

This eco-village consists of 54 hectares of land, including 24 hectares of meadow, and 30 buildings, including three saunas by the lake - and many kinds of possibilities for handicrafts, sports and other activities. Permaculture gardens, herb yards and greenhouses are in the making. The community produces much of their own food aiming at high self-reliance. The goal is to learn to sustain and conserve the traditional biodiversity of species in an otherwise cultivated rural environment. We are also reconstructing our energy systems. At the moment we are in an active planning phase to start the production of all our heating energy and electricity.

The Keuruu Eco-village is a meeting place for local people around us and people interested in our ideas. The eco-village is also a centre for courses in permaculture, environmental issues (eco-psychology, environmental education, etc.), rural skills and spiritual exercises (nature meditation, sacred dance, yoga etc.). We are able to offer board and lodging in our dormitories for 40 persons.

Many languages are spoken or understood by our inhabitants. Among these are Finnish, Swedish, English, German, Danish, Norwegian, Spanish and Esperanto. We have modern equipment for telecommunication.

The main organisations for our eco-village are the Association of the Keuruu Eco-village (founded in 1997, 30 members and 95 associated members) and the Co-operative of the Keuruu Eco-village (founded in 1997, 14 members). The Co-operative is responsible for the main economic activities in the eco-village. The Association owns the property.

People who want to get acquainted with our ideas are welcome to stay with us as guests of the Co-operative. People who want to live permanently in our village become members of the Association.

Contact:
Eco-Village of Keuruu
Liisa Jääskeläinen
Kivijärventie 300
42700 Keuruu
Finland

Tel: +358 14 73 65 71
Fax :   +358 14 73 65 53
e-mail: ekokyla@sci.fi

Ecolonie

We are a growing international community, which includes persons of all ages and nationalities. The association Ecolonie was founded in 1989 in Holland and currently includes over 50 members and supporters. We want to live in friendship with ourselves, Spirit and nature. We see ourselves as embodied in the living web of the Cosmos and we strive for a respectful relationship with one another, the Earth and all living beings.

We are concerned about the purity of water, air and soil. Thus we are seeking a simple lifestyle, without wasting natural resources and energy and without excessive consumption. In contrast to the isolation and splittering of city life, we want to establish a community of common respect and spiritual tolerance and support. We do not view conflicts as „war games" with winners and losers, rather we see them as a chance to learn more about ourselves and each other.

Through seminars, we want to establish a basis for demonstrating and sharing our ideas. We do not, however, believe in absolute „global guidelines" or truths. The world and its people are more diverse than the human spirit can ever conceive.

Ecolonie consists of 15 acres of land and forest, including a small lake and 5 spacious buildings. We are cultivating our biologic vegetable garden, renovating our living-, guest- and seminar buildings, beautifying our terrain and taking care of our chickens.

Ecolonie is situated in a very scenic area in the heart of the largest state forest in France on the west side of the Vosges mountains. The hilly, diverse countryside is the home for many rare plants and animals and invites one to hike, bike and horseback ride. The forest envelopes streams, gorges, waterfalls, ancient ritual sites, romantic villages and many beautiful, serene places. The region is bountiful and is famous in France as the „land of fountains". The resort cities Vital and Contrexeville are close.

At the moment, 8 residents are permanently living and working in the community, supported by short-term volunteers. We have some vacancies for residents. At any time of the year we can use helping hands, hearts and minds of volunteers. For volunteers or guests who want to participate in our community-life, we regularly organise Introductory Weeks. We are running a guest house and in summertime a natural camping area. Courses (arts, sprirituality and ecology) are mainly taking place in the holiday periods. We have a vegetarian kitchen, serving mostly home made products.

Contact:
Ecolonie
88260 Hennezel/Vosges
France

Tel: +33 32 90 700 27
Fax: +33 32 90 700 94

France
Montlaur
existing
eco-village

Les Sources

Founded at the end of 1993, our international association has acquired a 35 hectare land with 4 buildings; this land has its own spring. The acquisition has been financed by private loans and a bank loan. We expect to build additional houses according to our needs.

Each member, living on site, has to be financially independent; 7 people are permanently installed in our village and have outside activities. Possibilities are given to work in our village in agriculture or other traditional activities.

On the cultural and spiritual point of view, everybody has his own activity and his own way of thinking and living. We do not have any dogma or „guru".

The decisions are taken in common agreement during working groups. A „heart-meeting" has been created in order to give everybody the possibility to explain their problems and to listen to the other members of the village. During these meetings, we try to solve our conflicts.

We work every day together in common jobs, for instance: renewing or rebuilding, maintenance, garden, kitchen, firewood, planting... Our garden and our orchard are based on biological concepts and know how, including the principles of permaculture. Concerning energy, we have made the following investments:
• solar boiler
• solar cooker
• micro photo-voltaic power station installed on a pick-up truck
• photo voltaic power station
• biological waste water recycling

In the future we expect to install or to develop:
• a windmill for power supply
• a water turbine
• a car driven by electricity from photo voltaic
• a solar dryer for fruit...

Les Sources

We welcome people who want to live another kind of life. We accept new members after discussion about their motivation - and in common agreement. A financial contribution is required. Trainees are accepted for a longer period; they have to work 20 hours per week for common activities, and have to pay for meal and energy costs only.

Contact:
Les Sources
La Plage
11220 Montlaur
France

Tel: +33 468 24 02 18

Eco-village Vienne

The property comprises a small chateau, park land, 400 acres of organic farmland, forestry and substantial buildings suitable for future housing needs, Workshops, studios, offices, seminar rooms, together with sports and leisure facilities.

The trust plans to establish an eco community and technology centre which will not only be a working community but also cater for courses and conferences, eco holiday makers, work experience students, school parties and people coming to see the practical application of green technologies.

Featuring real life demonstrations of ecological living we aim to show visitors by example that it is quite feasible to find ways to make their own situations more sustainable.

A core group of people whose presence and activities will be a living example of real, practical and aesthetic work are needed to begin living at the Chateau during 1998.

In addition to the already considerable living spaces available for visitors, the existing housing comprises four spacious apartments, a large cottage and six studios. Later in 1998 some Austrian-built chalets, already on site, will be upgraded to provide an additional nine homes.

We are now looking for a core group who are independently responsible and can sustain themselves to come and live and work at the Chateau.

Nobody will be expected to buy their home or workspace at this eco-community. We will, however, ask that all people who live there or use the facilities make a financial investment by way of purchasing a block of shares and, thereafter, pay a nominal rent or user charge. We are looking at ways of offering help with this. Proposals are currently being put together by our bankers.

62

Eco-village Vienne

**France
Poitiers**
eco-village
initiative

It is vital to the successful running of the new eco-community that we have core group members with suitable experience in the areas of work detailed below:

Education
Catering
Bio Dynamic/Organic Farming
Gardening
Forestry
Office Administration
Course Facilitators
Permaculture
Herbalism

Alternative Technologies
Ecological Building
Motor Engineering
Plumbing
Electrical
Fish Farming
Crafts People
Therapies

Contact:
Eco-village Vienne
Gonda van Hal
EVV. BP 330
75625 Paris
Cedex 13
France

Tel: +33 145 65 95 27
Fax: +33 254 31 14 11
e-mail: Dominique.Boursin@wanadoo.fr

La Source d'Argens

At the dawn of the third millennium, the necessity of living in the full consciousness of an other reality of life is appearing, based on the respect and love of all life forms. Creation of an eco-village is for us building a life centre integrated in nature and attracting people ready to live according to their ideals. We are a group with open minds and common ideas. Our team is well-structured, solidly-linked, keen to achieve goals, dynamic, open to constructive relations between the residents and the outside world. All financial matters among the participants, the residents and the outside partners, will be guaranteed by the drawing up a charter and by legal transactions, clearly established by all founding members.

From a "bastide" (provencal farmhouse) called "La Source de Vie" in the village of Carcés, the potential for the creating an eco-village named "La Source d'Argens" evolved. It is a 6 hectares property located in a peaceful and harmonious setting - fit for recharging oneself. It is surrounded by vineyards, olive trees and woods. There is also plenty of water. The house is made of stones and can welcome 14 persons. There is a big shed. All these are made available for the creation of an eco-village. In all those living spaces, we are going to build individual dwellings, places for the reception, common premises for education, health, etc.

Furthermore, 7 hectares of flat land, totally irrigated by the water of the Argens river, is reserved for organic-dynamic agriculture and permaculture - an educational farm. There is also another piece of hilly and wooded land, 100 to 150 hectares, where we can create small and large structures with plenty of water. The training of young and older people in organic, bio-dynamic and permaculture is the goal of the educational farm.

There will be live-in partners and non-residents who will want to participate in the activities of this eco-village (homeopathic doctors, osteopaths, psychotherapists, dieticians, teachers, etc.) There will be partners ready to get involved in creating a fitness centre, cultural and artistic education, renewable energies, etc...

We plan a wood museum and selling of furniture, graphic arts, sculpture, painting and basketry. Later, we will build a research and communication centre for running workshops and conferences integrated into a regenerative and health centre. The research centre will specialise in agrobiology, ecology, alternative energies, various sciences, etc. and will have a forest project.

The will include:
• the excavation of a lake as a water reserve
• compost area
• breeding of Californians earth-worms
• an area for aromatic plants, for herbal medicine

Contact:
Association „La Source d'Argens"
Secrètariat National du Rèseau Francais des Eco-Villages
Madame Andrèe Fina
Bastide „la Source de Vie"
Chemin des Riaux
83570 Carcès
France

Tel: +33   4 94 04 34 32

Basisgemeinde Wulfshagenerhütten

The Basisgemeinde (base community) is a Christian community of
about 60 people - adults and children, married as well as single people

- situated in a little village in northern Germany. The community
started 25 years ago in southern Germany and moved to the buildings
of a former children's home in 1983 in order to establish a common
task. Since then members and guests of the community live and work
together in a loving and brotherly way.

We consider all the different kinds of work as equal in value and im-
portance, as they are all service and contribute to a common whole:
- the production of wooden toys and locomotion auxiliaries for kindergarten in our recently extended factory
- the distribution of our products and those of the Bruderhof communities all over Germany
- the biological farming co-operating with a neighbour farmer
- maintenance, administration, kitchen and our own kindergarten

Especially in a time of increasing unemployment, neoliberal orientation
and social disintegration, there is a need for alternatives. We believe that

Basisgemeinde Wulfshagenerhütten

everybody has gifts and abilities to share, and that taking part in daily work (as an essential part of human life) should be possible for all men. Therefore, we welcome everybody willing to share with us according to her/his abilities and needs.

Working in a different way is only one aspect of the new society the community is trying to work for. Longing for a world of peace and justice, of healed relationships among one another and with the earth, the community believes that it is the power of God and God´s love for the whole world that will lead people out of self-destruction and hope-lessness and build this new society. The community takes the Biblical promises and demands literally as the basic order of a new society. After many years of experience, the community testifies that the message of Jesus contained in the Sermon on the Mount, is the most revolutionary power there is, when it is taken seriously.

Following the example of the early Christians, all members of the com-munity share everything - money and possessions, time, responsibility for children and parents, political engagement. Together they carry the responsibility for the way of the community, and each step is taken in unity.

The community is engaged in ecological and political movement in relationship with its immediate neighbourhood. It is tied to a growing web of Christian communities all over the world. Living our faith is not only a matter of Sunday service, but the centre of all our activities. We welcome and invite everybody who wants to get to know our com-munity, to come and share our life with us for a short or long visit.

Contact:
Basisgemeinde Wulfshagenerhütten
Post Gettorf
24214 Wulfshagenerhütten
Germany

Tel: +49 43 46 50 44
Fax: +49 43 46 44 74

Lebensgarten

Living a social, cultural and ecological vision since 1985, Lebensgarten is:

- an international intentional community - a model for a new form of living together, filling the need for belongingness and social stability - and taking care of the environment
- a conversion project: from a national-socialistic (NAZI) ammunition worker's settlement to an ecological social centre, disseminating its experience of 13 years of a future and socially oriented way of life
- has a guest programmes of guided tours, exhibitions, lectures, artistic performances and participation in community life and rebuilding
- to live in harmony with nature and to transform a place of aggression and war activity into a peace community - based on creativity and tolerance

The community evolved out of approx. 20 dilapidated buildings, including a small hospital (now seminar house) and a large central building. It was originally built in 1939 and, since 1985, has been renovated by the members to be an eco-village with own row houses, shops and enterprises. Numerous working places have been created by various activities of the members and about one fourth found jobs in the immediate region.

In the educational facilities the knowledge which has been accumulated is disseminated in areas, such as Ecology, Healing, Healthy Building, Mediation and Personal Development (approx. 100 seminars and 3000 guests p.a.).

The organisation of this charitable association was founded in 1985, has presently 100 members and has an annual turnover of approx. DM 900 000 (US$ 500 000). Apart from the high level of neighbourliness, there are regular meetings for solving community problems, for circle dancing every morning and for different working groups. There are now over 150 persons living in the community - of different ages, social and professional backgrounds, different religions and objectives.

The organisations in our eco-village:

EDUCATION
Subjects:
- Connection Mind-Body-Soul
  (Zen, TaiChi)

DECISION-MAKING
BODIES
- Working Groups
- Steering Committee
  weekly meetings
- General Assembly of Members
          fortnightly

- Ecology (Baubilogie + Permaculture)
- Health
- Mediation (Conflict Resolution)
- Meditation
- Personal Development
- Suggestopedia (holsitic learning)

VEGETARIAN
NUTRITION

ECOLOGICAL
FACILITIES
- All-purpose gardens
- Co-generation (Electricity + Heat)
- Exhibition of energy saving systems
- Passive Solar Systems - glass roof
  and lean-to greenhouses
- Permaculture
- Solar Filling Station for 2 Electro-cars
- Solar Warm water Heating
- Rainwater collection

COMMUNAL
FACILITIES
Chapel
Craft-workshops
Kindergarten
Meditation rooms
Meeting places (Café)
Organic food co-op

CULTURAL LIFE
Art exhibitions
Circle dance daily
Concerts (international artists)
Lectures
Music recitals
Performances

CREATING BUSINESSES -
JOB CREATION
Biological Building Material Outlet
Bookstore
Computer-consultancy
Craft and Jewellery Shops
Ecological Architectural and Planning Office
Environmental Management and Consultancy
Global Eco-village Network (GEN-Europe) Office
Healing-practices for Natural healing, Homeopathy, Ergo-therapy
    and Sonology (Singing to support health)
Permaculture
School of Mediation
Seminar business: Organisation, Accommodation,   Course leaders

Germany Steyerberg
existing
eco-village

Lebensgarten

Key Dates

1938 - 39	Settlement built by Nazi regime
1945 - 77	British army camp
1977 - 85	Empty - left to ruin
1985 - 98	Conversion to eco-village: Lebensgarten
2000	15th. celebration within EXPO 2000

The first action that was taken was to move into this settlement, despite its ruinous state, and starting the renewal of the buildings one by one - from minimal resources except enthusiasm and commitment. Both physical and spiritual renewal was necessary because of more than 30 years of war activities in these walls radiated violence and inhuman realities. Actions chosen by consensus were re-building, insulating and renovating as well as meditation, conflict resolution and healing. 13 years later it looks like this:

Contact:
Lebensgarten Steyerberg e.V.
Ginsterweg 3
31595 Steyerberg
Germany

70

Tel.: +49 57 64 23 70
Fax: +49 57 64 25 78
e-mail: buero@lebensgarten.gaia.org
website: www.gaia.org

Mutter Erde

In Mother Earth (Mutter Erde) Community, people meet, whose desire for Truth, Eternity and Love has been awakened and who have decided to dedicate their lives to these goals. It is a place for those, who want to experience God directly in their heart and who aspire to achieve a lasting union between the Creator and the Creation. It is a Retreat Centre that wants to appeal to the human in a person and to show the unifying above all separation. Seifen's assignment has its foundation, firstly, in knowing that every being has a divine spark which means a deep respect for life in general and, secondly, in having the vision of world-brotherhood. Mutter Erde is a universal, non-denominational and multi-cultural meeting place for Religion, Science and Philosophy, applying fusion of the materialistic and spiritual aspects.
It is a place:

- of practical help in life for everyone who consciously wants to come Home, back to the Source, back to the true Self, to God
- of growing with each other and maturing individually
- where people might find their own responsible lifestyle and a personal experience of faith
- for people of all ages and denominations who want to live their ideals and make them come true
- especially for parents who treasure their children, having recognised the precious gift of family and wanting to support and preserve it

"Where there is peace in the family, there is peace in the world." (S.Sai Baba). So it is our intention to promote everything that serves unity in the manifold as well as beauty, grace and truth.

We experienced that every work done consciously and with devotion, brings us great blessings. Even though this attitude sometimes is hard to keep up, we are growing with every step. The everyday work is an initiation, step by step, giving us a deeper insight in life's mystery...

A firm rhythm of work and regular meditation gives a solid framework to our life. We practice adoring the Higher and supporting the Lower: i.e. the animals, plants and material things that we have been entrusted with or have created ourselves. Yet, everyone may stay loyal to his own path and practice the way of meditation or prayer which represents his personal nature. ˙

For short time visitors and those who come for the first time, we have established regular "Introductory Days". Also individual days of retreat or holidays are possible (call for details). Those who want to know more about life in a spiritual community may participate in an "Experience-week" (7 days; for details see our guide to programs). If you have in mind of joining a community or in participating intensively for a longer period, you may stay for a Quarter. The starting-day will be arranged individually.

Contact:
Mutter Erde e. V.
Holperstr. 1
57537 Forst-Seifen
Germany

Tel/Fax: +49 27 42 82 51

Sieben Linden

The Sieben Linden eco-village project aims at establishing a socially and environmentally progressive model settlement. The settlement is planned as a living and working space for 300 people and will be harmoniously adapted to the natural environment over a sustained period of time, enabling its inhabitants to live self-sufficiently and with self-responsibility.

In 1993, a Project Centre was established in Groß Chüden in the Altmark, in northern Saxon-Anhalt. The Centre consists of various living

facilities and work co-operatives as well as a nation-wide organisation: "The Friends of Ökodorf" and the project sponsor, the Housing and Settlement Co-operative: Ökodorf e.G.

In the spring of 1997, we finally found a site for the model settlement: Sieben Linden, 26 km south-west of the Project Centre in Altmark. At present, we are building the socio-ecological autonomous settlement Sieben Linden, located on a 22 hectare plot outside the village of Poppau. The property has forests and farm land as well as a barn and a house. In our work, we aspire to achieve the following goals:

Ecology: Sustainable settlement and economic structures with far-reaching, self-contained energy and material cycles. The creation and maintenance of the Biotop and its variety of plants and animals. Interconnection of agriculture and landscape features. Permaculture planning process.

Construction: Environmentally sound and future-oriented building methods, maximum potential for the inhabitants to self-build, organic architecture adapted to the landscape, the creation of meaningful spaces for living experiences, allowance for various life-style needs (families, singles, communes or shared housing, etc.).

Social organisation: Linking daily life and work, the integration of the individual and the community, self-responsibility in various life domains, direct communication and decision structures, collective living spaces for people of all age-groups and socio-economic backgrounds.

Economy: Decentralised economy with maximised self-sufficiency and direct local exchange via the development of agriculture, crafts, small businesses and cultural, social and medical services.

Local Region: Co-operation with surrounding villages through a long-term village and regional development plan which includes neighbourhood help, exchange of technical services as well as local trade, environmental protection and ecologically sound tourism.

The *Ökodorf Co-operative* ownes the Project Centre, an additional house and the settlement property Sieben Linden, near Poppau. Currently, the co-operative has 50 partner members (December, 1997) who are participating in the development of the project with their own capital and work. Seven of them form the new settlement group that is located at the Poppau site.

In 1991 the *Friends of the Ökodorf* (non-profit association) established themselves self as a group of supporters for the promotion of eco-village. Currently the group has 250 members. The bi-monthly newspaper and regular meetings disseminate information about the current state of the project. The organisation carries out public relations activities, networking with similar projects and offers a diverse, practical seminar program in co-operation with various experts and educational organisations.

The *Project Centre* is located on a 4,3 hectare farm in Groß Chüden. It has been the first point of crystallisation for all the various associated

Sieben Linden

initiatives along our way in conceiving the eco-village. It serves as the project's visitor centre and the co-ordinating facility for planning. Various companies have been established there and the centre has also been the stage for a number of valuable experiences that we have since been able to pass on to others. In the last years, over 70 adults and children have settled in the Centre itself and the immediate surrounding area.

The *Free School Altmark*, a branch of the eco-village project, sponsors a state-approved alternative school with a kindergarden for 36 children in Depekolk (11 kilometres from the project Centre and 17 kilometres from Poppau). The school's pedagogical approach is based on the idea that children must learn to trust their own inner growth capabilities and that a developing person's potential can only be lived out in his or her own time and tempo.

Guests and Visitors are welcome. If you want to visit us the first time, you must participate either in *the visitors day* once a month (the so-called PIT) or in one of the numerous seminars that we offer. You can also come as a working guest for two weeks every month - with free food and lodging, if you stay for a minimum of five working days. In any case, you must register in advance. During our winter break between December and March only private guests of community members are welcome.

Contact:
Ökodorf Sieben Linden
Dorfstr.4
38486 Poppau
Germany

Tel: +49 39 000 66 37
Fax: +49 39 01 82 942

"An hour of doing accomplishes more than years of procrastination". In the summer of 1979, more than 100 highly-committed people took this motto to heart and peacefully took over the desolate grounds of the former UFA-Film Studios in a very dense city area of Berlin. There they created a comprehensive work and living project, where art, work, housing, and daily life form together to create a new unit. Soon, it became an urban ecological community, hosting many innovative ideas

and concepts which were not only presented to the general public and discussed, but were practically implemented in the process of renovating the many dilapidated buildings.

From its beginning, the members of the UFA-Fabrik were concerned with ecological issues. Theyy were, for instance, one of the first groups in then West-Berlin to seperate and recycle all their wastes. The use of healthy materials was a stated aim, long before such materials were generally available.

Inspite of the large number of visitors, the area remains a reviving oasis in a major city - thanks to its gardens, green-roofs, an independent energy source and a rain water-collecting system. This is why we like to refer to it sometimes as an urban eco-village. The recently installed

UFA-Fabrik

solar panel system produces enough electricity to supply the whole UFA-Fabrik! An exhibition explains these and other projects to the interested visitor.

Today, the resident community consists of 50 members (from age one month to 90 years), about 120 employees, and receives more than 200.000 visitors per year. The UFA-Fabrik has a world-wide reputation as a multi-cultural site for innovative social, cultural and ecological lifestyles. During its first six years, the UFA-Fabrik functioned without receiving any subsidies. After years of discussion with the Berlin Senate, a lease was finally signed. The rent was raised, but this gave the UFA-Fabrik long-term security as well as the possibility to obtain government support for certain ecolopgical and cultural projects.

Two theatres are open all year-round for stage productions: The large theatre seats about 400 and the historical movie theatre, known today as Varieté Salon, seats about 200. Everything from cabaret, comedy, world music, lectures, dance theatre to children´s programmes and circus revues is presented here. On alternative summers the UFA-Fabrik hosts an International Theatre Festival. The International Culture Centre (IKS) is a member of the Trans Europe Halles Network, an organisation of independent European cultural institutions that all are situated in former factory buildings.

This centre offers various public sport and leisure classes, ranging from parents romping and dancing with their 2-year-olds to senior citizens practising Chinese Qi-Gong meditation. Aikido and Tai Chi skills, workshops for dance, afro-drumming, Brazilian percussion and more are offered regularly. The Animal Farm for children keeps animals seldom seen in the dense city blocks: pigs, chickens, geese, ferret, and ponies.

The premises, 16.000 square metres (approx. 4 acres) is divided into various areas. The visitor can find a bakery and the UFA-shop for organically grown products. The Café Olé, with its summer garden terrace, intices a pleasurable visit for people of all ages and nationalities.

Contact:
UFA-Fabrik
Viktoriastraße 10-18
12105 Berlin Süd
Germany

Tel: +49 30 75 50 30
e-mail: info@ufafabrik.de
web page: www.ufafabrik.de

ZEGG

ZEGG is the German abbreviation for „Zentrum für Experimentelle Gesellschaftsgestaltung", Centre for Experimental Cultural Design. ZEGG is an international meeting point for questions of a future worth living. It is a study centre for the co-operation with nature, for questions of autonomy and survival, for new solutions in love and for the creation of a network for a humane world. ZEGG experiments in ‚community' as a model for life and a building ground for a concrete utopia.

It was started in 1991 at a 45 acre site in Belzig, 80 km south-west of Berlin, as the result of a network growing since 1978. The community consists of about 75 adults and children.

Work is done in all areas that need change: the heating and hot water supply are run by an environmentally friendly wood chip heating system; the sewage is cleared by a purification plant using marsh vegetation; both systems were planned and installed by businesses within ZEGG. The garden supplies the community and the guests with organic food to a great extent.

In order to increase communication among each other the ZEGG community uses the ritual of the ‚forum'. This creates the necessary transparency and trust for living together. In the past it turned out to be an essential practise which effectively guaranteed that the group could sail through every internal crisis, unharmed, since 1978. Beside the forum the community uses music, theatre, festivities, meditation and other various forms and rituals to come together.

The ZEGG residents live together in small households of different sizes. Each person is responsible for their financial situation. There are some companies on the compound, partially Active in eco-technology or in servicing areas. Some of the members are employed in these companies or at ZEGG Ltd. Other community members do free lance work. For the various areas of responsibility there are committees such as conferences and seminars, property, finances, social issues, public relations and media, children etc. Important decisions are prepared by the committee and then presented to the plenary where they are decided by consensus.

ZEGG is open for all who are interested. Sunday afternoon from 3pm to 5pm visitors are free to just drop in, starting at 3pm. Get-to-know weekends also offer an opportunity to have deeper insight into ideas and get to know the place better. The big conventions at Easter, Whit weekend, Summer Camp, Fall Camp and New Year are festivals and networking hubs for both new visitors and old friends. There are price reductions for youth and students.

Contact:
ZEGG GmbH
Rosa-Luxemburg-Strasse 89
14806 Belzig
Germany

Tel: +49 33 84 15 95 10
Fax: +49 33 84 15 95 12
e-mail: infopost@zegg.dinoco.de
web site: www.ecovillage.org/germany/zegg

Dolphin Community

The Dolphin Community - Ways to God - stands for the connection between Heaven & Earth - Spirituality & Matter - Vision & Implementation. Based on this principle, we live together in a community through spiritual diversity, common chanting, hiking and biking tours, nursing children, decision making and conflict resolution, without owning a common place to live at. We try to learn from other people's experiences and attempt to share our own experiences through our Eco-village Institute consultancy by looking for communities and references, with the aim of serving the next in line. We are currently engaged in setting up a hospital in India, where the poor would receive free medical treatment. It is possible to grow up to some 15 members including children, and later on to get integrated into a bigger unit such as an Eco-village. As a potential first step, we have founded Regional Talent-Exchange Society (a development on the LETSystem based on the talents of the society members). The identification of our housing is something we leave to divine inspiration, and it will most probably be in the province of Baden, between Heidelberg and Basel, with perhaps land enough for permaculture. Financing can be solved through contributions from the already existing solidarity fund of community projects in Northern Germany, or by establishing a Southern German fund.

Contact:
Delphin-Gemeinschaft
Karl-Heinz Meyer
Goethestr. 21
79650 Schopfheim
Germany

Tel/Fax: +49 762 26 53 02

Hare Krishna Community

We have been farming here in the Bavarian Forest since the beginning of the 1980's, not only as an attempt at an alternative lifestyle, but as an integral part of an holistic approach to dealing with the sociological and ecological challenges confronting us. We see ourselves as an eco-village initiative. Some day we will get there. Everyone knows how difficult it is to live in an independent and consistent way. To produce one's own foodstuffs is the first step, and to avoid tractors, for instance, relying only on oxen is coming closer to the goal. We are also planning an oxen-driven mill. What was a common every-day way of living is now usually considered as a denial of our so-called modern technological advancement. Anyone who takes an honest look, and sees where today's society is headed, must be interested in a practical alternative. To this end, we are attempting to follow a lifestyle that practically embodies these principles.

As members of the local organic farmers' association (Biokreis Ostbayern e.V.), our farming work falls within the parameters of their strict guidelines. Our 21 hectares are mainly pasture for our cows and bulls, and a part of it is used for vegetables, grains and flowers for our own use. About four dozen young people between the ages of 25 and 35 -

Hare Krishna Community

and among them a few families with children - make up our community. 25 are resident on our land and another 20 or so live in the neighbouring village, but are closely connected to the project. We plan to build 3 or 4 new houses, especially for the couples with families, but as yet we have not got planning permission.

On a voluntary basis each individual contributes to the project according to their means. The most important consideration is the consciousness behind the endeavours, and the interest to participate and learn in an interactive way. All members of the community are independent and responsible for themselves and may leave the community when they like.

If you would like to participate, you should be ready and happy to live vegetarian, free from intoxicants, during your stay. We ask that visitors to retain an open mind for the principles of Krishna consciousness (Bhakti-Yoga). Our spiritual practices are based on the teachings of the Vedic literature, especially the Bhagavad Gita. If you are interested in understand more about this, we suggest you visit your local Hare Krishna centre.

The easiest way for interested persons to get a real picture of our farm community, is to experience it for themselves by stopping by for a visit (over the weekend, for example). We recommend those who wish to spend extended stays with us, begin with some short visits, so that we can get to know each other, before mutually committing ourselves.

Contact us at:
Nrsimha Kshetra - Hare Krishna Farm Community
Zielberg 20
94118 Jandelsbrunn
Germany

Tel: +49 85 83 316
Fax: +49 85 83 16 71

ÖkoDorf Initiative Osnabrück

The project was started by the secondary school teacher Ebba Ehrnsberger and a group of five people, including the architect Rolf Brinkmann and the engineer Aloys Graw, in the fall of 1993. The goal was to build an eco-village in or close to Osnabrück (north Germany). About 50 persons responded to newspaper advertisement. From this core group, a working committee was formed having the task of setting up a detailed brief for an ecological community. An energy concept was worked out by Energy Graw, a concept for waste disposal by AWA and a water and decentralised sewage proposal by Cyclos. We are still discussing the urban design, the landscape planning and the "social" concept, but we know we want acceptance of senior citizens, the handicapped and foreigners and the physical integration of offices, practices, shops and a café.

An association of interested people was founded in 1997, obtaining non-profit status in 1998. The legal form for the implementation of the project will be quite complicated because of German law. A Genossenschaft (i.e. a Co-operative) will take over the building and maintenance of the roads, paths, squares, and infrastructure like gas, water and sewage as well as the community building.

The site plan avoids sub-division but dictates large building "windows", as we are calling them. The large plots can be

ÖkoDorf Initiative Osnabrück

taken over by property owner groups, (maybe 4-8 families) This way there can be many different solution, having the most flexibility legally. The more than 300 originally interested people came from far and wide, from Bavaria and from California. Now we are down to 80, but only 24 committed members of the Co-operative.

In the meantime, we have found a plot of land of 2 ha being part of a former army barracks. A subdivision plan according to our own concept is in the process of being legally cleared. The final plan includes 45 to 50 housing units, mainly terraced, one common house with café, one grocery store and offices. Natural gas fired co-generation is suggested for electricity and heating. Rainwater will be used for toilet flushing, cold water inlet of washing machines and for garden watering. The houses will be of low energy standard (50 kwh/m2/year) and will be constructed of natural and healthy materials. Passive solar gain will be "built in".

In the village there will be no motor vehicle traffic; the cars will be parked centrally at the entrance to the settlement. There will be lots of green and as less as possible of the ground will be sealed. Waste water will be treated in a septic tank and afterwards pumped horizontally through a wetland-bed. Any left-over sludge can be used for fertilising farm land in the area. We plan to start construction in 1998.

Contact:
OekoDorf, Rolf Brinckmann
Friesenhof 27
49078 Osnabrück
Germany

Tel/Fax: +49 541 44 59 41
e-mail: OekoDorf@aol.com
website: http://members.aol.com/OekoDorf/index.htm

Elikon Institute is co-operating with the centre for transformational architecture and living-forms in Worpswede, Germany. In winter 1993, Harald Jordan and Tina Agiorgiti-Jordan both received a strong, inner impulse to begin realising a vision which they have been carrying for many years. The vision entails creating a place, an eco-village, of learning, practice, exchange, deepening and sharing, in the service of raising human consciousness and integrating human living-space and living-form harmoniously within the natural environment.

After a year's intensive search, a piece of land about 12 500m^2 was found on the island of Evia (Euboia), matching our requirements. It was an agricultural estate, abandoned for decades, on a terraced plateau, overlooking the Aegean sea. The estate contained rich vegetation, including vines, oak, chestnut, olive, fig, lemon, almond, plum and

mulberry trees. There were two running water sources. The central house- at least 200 years old, was partly destroyed by a fire and parts of it needed demolishment. Minimal requirements for living were set up by a talented German ecological architect. No sooner had they finished clearing the old house and set up a provisory kitchen, people started showing up. They came from Athens, Germany, United States, England and Scotland (Findhorn). Some were there out of curiosity, some

Elikon Institute

to learn, others to help and share the vision. Since 1994 the project has been having non-stop visitors.

Elikon is reachable by jeep, courageous sturdy car or by foot. Ammenities like electricity and telephone are available at Akteon town- approx. 50 people, 3 kilometers away (20 mins. walking distance). Post comes once a week to Akteon. There are two swimming places nearby, about 20 minutes on foot. One is a secluded beach, the other, is a rock formed area with cathedral-like caves which one can swim into or re- treat. Dolphins and eagles are often seen. Daily life is attuned to the natural light rhythms. Our material furnishing are kept volantarily sim- ple. Presently all guests live in furnished, large Sahara tents (4m dia- meter) supported by old olive trees trucks. Though constructed for 8 persons, these accommodate only 2 guests.

The group are working the land very cautiously due to its purity and using geomantical knowledge. In view of their own sustainability, they have been introducing forest-farming principles from Robert Hart and permaculture techniques from Bill Mollison and David Holm-

gren. Also they have had astounding success with the natural farming methods of Masinobu Fukuoka, under the guidance of one of his students, living in northern Greece. They also learned a lot from the local people's domestic gardens, architec- ture and village design. The site has a micro climate, due to the mountains surround- ing the plateau and the sea. Often in summer, there are light cloud formations du- ring parts of the day. This makes life and work bearable in the hot summer months.

Main wind comes from North and South and are very strong here. It has been a challenge keeping the mulch on the ground!

Though Elikon was originally intended for the summer use, it is now in the process of planning and building retreats and sustainablitiy amenities for the winter months also, so that it can become a real eco-village.

Materials end up costing three times more due to the conditions of the road and to the difficulty of transport. This is one of the reasons why they are looking into more lighter and economical building methods. In the coming years, they envision using solar and wind energy for our needs. They have been experimenting with building techniques for the Mediterranean climate and have been successful in combining modern knowledge with traditional Greek village architecture. In the first three years, they have had abundant support and inspiration from our guests and students, from visiting professors and groups from the architectural departments of Oldenburg, Nienburg and Kassel in Germany.

Since the first ‚pioneering' days, the vision is steadily manifesting. Up to present, Elikon in Greece has been financed by its founders. This was necessary for the beginning stages. In view of mobilising the further potential of this unique place, they are open for support in the following ways:

- financial support in pre-financing individual retreats in exchange for free stays at Elikon GR
- financial support and donations for special experimental building projects as is the building of the library, sanctum, seminar room, sanitary spaces, water-system and solar/wind energy systems

Greece
Evia
eco-village
initiative

Elikon Institute

- practical knowledge in ecological building techniques and passive energy systems
- practical knowledge in sustainablility, growing and preserving food
- practical knowledge in creating infrastructures within Elikon
- practical knowledge in supporting the neighbouring village sustaining itself and keeping the natural surroundings intact
- networking and exchange of experience with other communities and other independent settlements or individuals in the greater area, in view of a larger initiative (land is presently for sale)
- long-term guests, new members and focalisers

Elikon in Greece, is steadily becoming a place of inspiration, learning, experiment, inter-diciplinary exchange, empowerment, deepening and practice-field for new models of living. Although it is visited mostly by non-Greeks, they also envision it as playing a supporting role, in raising environmental and spiritual consciousness in the area of Greece. Transformation is the leap from having to being, from producing to creativity, from knowing to wisdom, from believing to certainty, from scarcity to abundance.

Contact:
Tina Agiorgiti-Jordan
Poste Restante, Akteon,
Evia, Greece

or

Elikon Institute
Tina Agiorgiti-Jordan
Bauernreihe 8a
27726 Worpswede
Germany

Tel: +49 47 92 36 47
Fax: +49 47 92 47 43

Gyürüfü was started in 1991 and now has over 20 permanent residents throughout the year. A larger number are still building their houses. It is situated in Southwest Hungary, in a hilly area called Zselic, with narrow deep valleys and pastures and surrounded by managed forests. Due to the lack of accommodation on the Gyürüfü project itself, most of the people involved live in the town of Ibafa right next to it. The offices for the project are also based there.

There has been a village at Gyürüfü long ago which had fallen into total disrepair over the last forty years due to the governments policy

of centralisation. Most of the buildings were totally unusable except for the materials which can be scavenged. One of the problems faced by the initiators has been the long hard winters which delayed construction of the access road considerably.

The Gyürüfü Foundation searches for sustainable alternatives to present day development practices. It is assumed that the principles of ecological lifestyle and the application of co-operative methods and appropriate technologies can be organised into one comprehensive, integrated and holistic scheme meeting all the needs of human existence without upsetting the natural balance. The principal aim is to build up a human scale community pattern which gives high priority to mu-

Gyürüfü

tual co-operation, personal contacts and understanding without giving up individual freedom and dignity.

The Gyürüfü community is a self-organising, autonomous, independent group of very different people who are linked by a comon goal of living in an ecological community. Gyürüfü does not highlight any religious or spiritual aspect, and people here tend to think that these types of issues belong to the private realm of every person. One of the main contributions has been a special emphasis on information technology and tele-communication in order to offset more harmful technologies. The distribution of manual and intellectual labour takes place not only among the different people, but within the activities of individuals as well.

Problem solving is usually done by consensus; in the lack of it, a majority vote is applied (this seldom happens). There is a clear distinction between the foundation as a legal body and the community as the people actively participating in the project. Much effort has been put into the development of a set of by-laws, which still needs final endorsement. The community has no appointed leader, the foundation and the companies do.

The most important aspect of the actual building and settling was that of organic development. This meant a gradual, step-by-step construction and building inside the area, allowing enough space for redesign, following the changing needs and accumulating experience. Earth sheltering has many advantages in that insulation properties are excellent and the indoor climate is stable - cool in summer and warm in winter. The first phase of housing has in fact now been completed and there are four finished houses on the site. Domes are popular for earth covered buildings as they have an inherent strength due to their shape which can support the weight of earth on top.

The common house, an ambitious earth sheltered domed building, is now finished and is used as residence for workers and inhabitants who have not yet finished their own buildings. There is a central hall in the common house. Funding for this project came also from Gaia Trust in Denmark and the European Union who have strongly supported Gyürüfü with infrastructural and construction funding. The worn footwear is hung by the builders in true Hungarian custom to show time and effort used on building and is said to bring luck.

Within the village boundaries, car traffic is prohibited with the exception of transporting heavy loads, or aged or ill persons. Alternatives for locomotion can be bicycles, horseback, buggies, etc. Some machinery

Gyürüfü

is allowed for land management, forestry, construction work, etc. Methods are being developed to adapt the principles of permaculture design to a temperate continental climate as well. Forestry, agriculture, architecture, traffic, handicrafts, industry and culture will create one indivisible, complex system.

Contact:
Andrea & Bela Borsos
Gyurufu Alapitvany Foundation
Arany Janos utca 16
7935 Ibafa
Hungary

Tel/Fax: +36 73 35 43 34
e-mail: gyurufu@gyurufu.zpok.hu

Sólheimar is an eco-village in southern Iceland about 85 km from the capital, Reykjavík. Founded in 1930, it may well be the oldest village in the Global Eco-village Network. Today, the village of 250 hectares has about 100 inhabitants, living in 38 houses and apartments, with 5 more houses currently under construction.

Sólheimar was inspired by the philosophy of Rudolph Steiner, using biodynamic farming and being one of the first such farms in Scandinavia. Anthroposophical architecture and other elements help to ensure full participation of all community members, taking into account the special needs and skills of each individual.

Sólheimar occupies a uniquely fortunate position with regard to available natural resources. All of the area heating and hot water is generated by natural hot springs. The first hot spring, which was capped before the settlement in 1930, provides nine liters of 90° C water per second, and a second hot spring provides 12 liters of 90° C water per second. This natural hot water, along with favourable sunshine and rainfall, a moderate maritime climate and good soil are great sources of natural wealth.

From the beginning Sólheimar has focused on cultivating the individual- and the environment, for example: waste is sorted and organic ma-

Sólheimar

terials placed in compost which are then used as fertiliser; cardboard paper is used in reforestation; paper is used to manufacture cards and various handicrafts; excess candle wax is collected from individuals as well as restaurants in Reykjavík and used to make new candles; old clothing is utilised in weaving. Today, about 65% of waste products from Sólheimar are recycled on the grounds, in addition to an increasing amount of waste from other sources that is recycled to create products of value.

Sólheimar has developed a broad-based range of industries and activities, and include the following:

- Ölur Reforestation Centre - It is the only organic reforestation centre in Iceland. It is currently around 120 hectares in size, where there are grown 500.000 trees annually, of which 15.000 are planted on Sólheimar's own land.
- Sunna Nursery - Organic greenhouse cultivation: products include tomatoes, cucumbers and bell peppers. Outdoor cultivation includes potatoes, various types of cabbage and carrots. The community could produce ample additional food by simply building more greenhouses, and in fact, the construction of a 1300m² greenhouse has recently been completed.
- Vala Grocery & Art Gallery - Organic vegetables, manufactured items as well as handicrafts and art pieces created by residents are sold here, open daily during the summer.
- Candle making - Production is entirely handmade from beeswax and recycled candles. Wax sculptures are also created.
- Farming - The community raises calves, chickens, goats and horses.
- Brekkukot guest accommodation is open all year, the two guest houses have accommodation for up to 34 in made-up beds. There are 7 single and 13 double rooms; eight rooms have private bath-

rooms. Both houses have good cooking facilities. Cooked food is also available. There are also three apartments available with facilities that include bedroom, kitchenette, bath and living room. Brekkukot is the first guest house in Iceland that received an official certification as a sustainable travel service. Other guest houses within 15 - 20 km from Sólheimar can ccommodate over 300 people.

Today the garden displays seven sculptures by as many artists. It gives an overview of Icelandic sculpture during the years 1900 -1950. The garden will be completed in the year 2000 when a total of 10 sculpture will be displayed.

- Activities - Sólheimar has an athletic club, choir, theatre group, gymnasium and an outdoor swimming facility all year round, with hot tub and steam bath. There are also fine walking paths.

- Eco-village Training Centre - which amongst other things offers courses on permaculture and educational days.

The Sólheimar community is self-sufficient, and has both worldly and spiritual aims. The core idea is to create harmony of traditions with new technologies that responsibly utilise natural resources, thereby handing over to future generations a planet in balance with itself that can provide the same opportunities for individual and communal self-fulfilment. Self-sufficient communities such as Sólheimar are leaders in discovering natural solutions to environmental problems facing the world today.

Contact:
Sólheimar at Grímsnes
801 Selfoss
Iceland

Tel: +354 486 44 30
Fax: +354 486 44 83
e-mail: solheima@smart.is
web site: http://smart.is/solheimar

Damanhur

Damanhur was founded in 1979 by a group of people inspired by Oberto Airaudi's idea of uniting a spiritual philosophy with practical everyday life. It is now a federation of several villages and communities: Damjl, Etulte, Tentyris, Rama and Valdajmil. They are situated in the Valchiusella area, a pre alpine valley in the Piemonte in northern Italy.

The Federation now numbers over 400 full time members and 300 others who live nearby and take part in its activities. Residents are of all ages and come from all over the world, allthough at the moment the majority is still Italian.

Damanhur offers different levels of membership according to the level of involvement each person chooses, from full-time residency to people who live all over the world, but visit us regularly. Damanhur has several centres in Italy, one in Berlin and maintains contacts with spiritual groups world-wide. Every year, thousands of people, especially from abroad, come to Damanhur to study and research, or simply to share everyday life.

Damanhur has more than 40 economic activities, artistic workshops, a daily newspaper to stimulate debate and exchange of ideas, a Constitution, a currency (Credit, value in Feb. 1998 = 1,400 Liras), internal schools, elective bodies, an open university offering seminars in many fields of social, artistic and spiritual research.

At the centre of the Damanhurian spiritual path is the expression of the individual's artistic creativity. Creative expression serves the purpose of blessing time and space, an idea which has materialised in the Temple of Mankind, a concrete collectively-built edifice in which all Damanhurians have participated. The Temple of Mankind has made Damanhur widely known. It is an underground building, rich in works of art and built completely by hand by the members of the Federation. It symbolically represents the inner rooms of every human being. Walking in its halls and corridors corresponds to an inner journey deep inside oneself. Just as in the Renaissance, the construction of the Temple of Mankind has given impulse to the creation of artistic and handicraft workshops for which Damanhur is now known and appreciated all over the world. Glass, mosaic, painting, sculpture, ceramics, embossed metal...

The society of Damanhur is interested in creating a sustainable way of living and consider our planet a living being to respect and preserve. In Damanhur nobody smokes and smoking is not allowed even outdoors as a form of respect - not only for humans, but also for plants, animals and the natural environment.

Since the very first day of its foundation, Damanhur has being recycling its waste, farming organicly and looking for eco-compatible ways of living, of producing and of developing its settlements.

The businesses of Damanhur are bringing new life to the limited economy of Valchiusella, a valley which has never before enjoyed a prosperous economic development. The members of Da-

Damanhur

manhur are also actively involved in the valley councils, where 13 members have been elected on Damanhur's own political party and now sit in 4 different village councils, co-operating with ideas and projects to the social and economic development of the whole valley. The social structure has been refined over 20 years, creating a People with a strong national identity and a unique style of life. A division of Harper & Collins, one of the world's largest publishing houses, has published the first book in English on the Federation, called: Damanhur: the Real Dream, Thorsons Books, 1998.

Damanhur's governing bodies:
- *the Federal Council* - three members elected every six months. They have a spiritual function, verify long term plans and determine the general direction of the Federation. They interact constantly with the other bodies of the Federation, in order to create dynamic confrontation.
- *The College of Justice* - three members elected every year.
- *Community bodies* include the Presidents of the Communities - elected every year. The rules for elections are established by each community and each community enjoys a wide degree of autonomy.
- *The Council of the Representatives of the Homes*, and
- *The Citizens Assembly*

Contact:
International Relations, Federation of Damanhur
10080 Baldissero C.se (TO)
Italy

Tel:	+39 124 51 22 26
Fax:	+39 124 51 21 84
e-mail:	welcome@damanhur.it
web site:	www.damanhur.it

The Fondazione Bhole Baba, an eco-village of the Italian network R.I.V.E. (Rete Italiana Villaggi Ecologici), became a spiritual centre in 1979 at the suggestion of Babaji, Mahavatar of the Himalayas. We have about five hectares of land, which we work according to organic principles, after having experienced the biodynamic agriculture of Rudolf Steiner for many years. We also have two cows that give us milk and cheese.

Thousands of people have experienced life at the ashram, coming to purify themselves, to receive the divine light, to learn a style of life connected with nature. We are able to give hospitality to 35 - 40 people. The ashram includes a rich library with books on spirituality, agriculture and ecology.

Life in the ashram is organised in a natural rhythm: waking up at sunrise, prayers at the dhuni (sacred eternal fire) and at the temple, karma yoga (the work offered to the Divine unconditionally); in the fields and to maintain the buildings. During the last meeting of R.I.V.E., Panos Manikis became a guest of the Foundation Bhole Baba. He is a very

Italy
Cisternino
existing
eco-village

Fondazione Bhole Baba

pure man, united with the rhytmes of the Universe and has taught us the principles of natural agriculture. We are vegetarian and we want to develop solar energy. We strive to live in harmony with our Mother Earth so that everybody is able to find the capacity to regenerate his physical and inner energies in himself.

Our community is able to give hospitality to people open to the Divine and willing to work together. It is our aim to contribute to heigthening the consciousness of the area in which we live, through the example of how we respect all human beings and our Mother Earth.

Contact:
Fondazione Bhole Baba
Lisetta Carmi
Casella Postale 56
72014 Cisternino (BR)
Italy

The Upacchi Co-operative was founded in March 1990, and then acquired the abandoned village of Upacchi, in the province of Arezzo (Tuscany). The 16 houses were sold to private persons, the grounds and wood (80 ha of wood, 20 ha of agricultural land) are property of the Co-operative, to which also the inhabitant of the village belong. At the moment, about half of the houses have been rebuilt ecologically, and are inhabited by Italian and German families. A few houses are still to be sold. The Co-operative has also created infrastructure, like a water pipe, a biological waste water treatment system and have had electricity and telephone lines installed. We started with 12 sq.m of sun collectors and are slowly working up to 70 sq.m. We have some photovoltaic panels and we use an ecological generator for the rest of the electricity. Otherwise, there is a lot of passive solar systems built in during the renovations.

The main activities of the inhabitants are crafts (carpentry, mud building techniques, electric installations), biological farming, therapy and teaching (outside the village). For the future, more educational and ecological work is planned to be done in the village itself. The type of

Upacchi

activities envisaged in the future are: Building 30%, agriculture 20%, consulting in environmental matters, ecological techniques and biological agriculture 50%.

The social organisation consists of:
- the members assembly of the Co-operative Agricola Upacchi (minimum 3 persons)
- the administrative body with a manager and a president elected for 2 years
- plus two task forces for special social or legal problems

Contact:
Eva Lotz
Villaggio Upacchi
52031 Anghiari (AR)
Italy

Tel: +39 575 74 93 23
Fax: +39 575 74 93 22
web site: www.ecovillages.org/italy/upacchi

The late medieval village of Torri Superiore (14th Century) is a little jewel of popular architecture, completely built in stone in the Ligurian hinterland near Ventimiglia (Imperia), a few kilometres from the sea and the French border. All one building, with many different levels connected by narrow passageways and staircases, a magical labyrinth of rooms and terraces was created. It was abandoned at the beginning of this century. In 1989 the *Associazione Culturale Torri Superiore* started the project to preserve the entire structure and make it a permanent community and a cultural centre open to others.

We are a group of people who are searching for a more rewarding life, based on the principles of co-operation, solidarity and respect for people, for nature and for the surrounding environment. Different as we are from each other, we are held together by the dream to revive this se-

ductive microcosm in harmony with the material and spiritual needs of each one of us. Today, eight members of the group live permanently in Torri and take care of the house and of the work in progress.

We are planning to restore all the Buildings and use a large part of the village, 50%, as an open community centre, owned by the „Assosia-zone", a non-profit organisation. The members will live in 20 little apartments, privately owned, and take care of cultural and social activities full-time, as well as organic agriculture and international work camps.

Torri Superiore

We are members of Arci-Nova, Legambiente, Greenpeace, Amnesty International and GEN-Europe

If you are interested in knowing more about us and our project:
Contact:
Ass. Culturale Torri Superiore
via Torri Superiore 5
18039 Ventimiglia
Italy

Tel/Fax: +39 184 21 52 90
e-mail: torrisup@rosenet.it
web site: www.rosenet.it/torrisup/indexen.htm

Global Village Bagni di Lucca

Italy
Lucca
eco-village
initiative

In Bagni di Lucca, we are creating an ecological global village which will connect us to the larger planetary village in which to carry out all health, cultural and religious programmes which we feel should be the roots of a true human culture. A village of global health and education which will permit us to heal our body, mind and soul - utilising the best that science, art and culture has to offer. An open space for all realities in which respect for nature and our bodies will be in first place. All toxic and polluting substances (detergents, medicines, food) will be banned, only natural and ecological materials will be used and a great attention will be given to the use of natural or recycled materials. Bagni di Lucca (The City of Waters) is an ideal environment for the realisation of this project of planetary culture. Its ancient cultural tradition, beauty, ideal climate and uncontaminated ecosystem are its strong points.

The name „City of Waters" is given by the richness of its thermal waters, judged to be among the best in Europe. The thermal Spa of Bagni di Lucca has more than twenty different thermal springs which have various different therapeutic and esthetic properties. The Global Village Association has presented to the Commune of Bagni di Lucca a detailed project for a Global Village and have signed a twenty year contract for the rent and management of two main buildings and of the thermal complex. This project is unique in its kind because the „new village" is growing inside the „old village" of Bagni di Lucca which has a very old tradition of culture and health, dating back to the Roman Empire. In the valley of Bagni di Lucca, there are an incredible variety of rare medical herbs - and tales of healers, fairies and angels of the hot springs abound. This Global Village will experiment the union between the old and the new culture by working in two directions: in a simple introductory way with the local establishments and residents, who are very open to new ideas, and in a deeper way with its own inner participants.

The Global Village project is culturally and economically backed up by a series of non-profit associations which operate in various fields but with analogous goals. Among these are the Club of Budapest, an international association founded with the objective of promoting a

Global Village Bagni di Lucca

planetary consciousness, the cultural-scientific association Cyber Holistic Research, the Lama Gangchen World Peace Foundation which works towards non-formal education and world peace, and Radio Pace(the Peace Radio) - a radio station in Italy for positive news.

The project in Bagni di Lucca intends to use the buildings of the thermal spa to create a citadel of new planetary culture. The main activities at the village are:

- global Education; education towards peace, ecology, training of doctors and therapists, teachers and students
- holistic Medicine oriented towards prevention and global health
- planetary culture; conferences, concerts, exhibits and films on the themes of the new culture
- development of human potential; meditation, Yoga, Tai-Chi, psychosomatic and psychotherapy
- ecological and cultural development and maintenance; of the area's natural resources
- art and Creativity; music, art, dance and creativity for the new man

Contact:
Global Village of Bagni di Lucca
Amala Montecucco
Bagni di Lucca
55021 Lucca
Italy

Tel/Fax: +39 58 38 64 04
e-mail: village@cln.it
web site: http://www.urra.it/cyber/wwwvilla.html

The EVA-Lanxmeer project in Culemborg is a typical example of how originally an initiative of a group of citizens becomes a partnership between them and the local authorities. The whole project aims more at ecological goals than the technicalities of producing building units for a normal settlement. Planning is in its final stages and the building phase is soon to start.

EVA

The site which is directly adjacent to the railway station in Culemborg was formerly a water catchment area and still part of it is used for pumping water from 150 meter below for drinking water supply for this town of 50.000 inhabitants. It has quite a few trees at the periphery of the site and a windbreak of poplars near the water catchment area, where there are also well spaced fruit trees in an orchard. A landscape design has been done, according to permaculture principles. By the end of 1998, the building of the first 50 dwellings will start.

On a site of 24 hectares, an ecological town quarter and a city farm are to be developed as an example of urban permaculture. A multiplicity of different designs for the housing - in a dense area beside the railway - are to be accompanied by various other functions in order to bring work-places, recreation, transport, manufacturing and living areas together in such a way that each element supports the other. Reduction or elimination of air, water and soil pollution as well as noise and unnecessary garbage is the aim of the settlement initiators. Further aims are the integration of social aspects, healthy food production, re-cycled materials, generation of alternative energy and water re-use and re-cycling systems. The building programme is not set but roughly aims at creating:

- 100 flats as a mixed residential area
- 60 one-family houses or row houses
- 40 zero-energy high density dwellings
- 3000 sq.m. of offices and shops for ecologically oriented projects, producers, planners, manufacturers and firms
- 3500 sq. m. of office and exhibition space for the Association for Baubiologie of the Netherlands
- 1000 sq. m. of office and exhibition space for the ecological centre of the E.V.A. Foundation

This project has been initiated mainly by Marleen Kaptein whose push and action has not only started the idea of an urban eco-village, but she was also the initiator of the EVA Foundation. EVA stands for Educatie, Voorlichting en Advies (Education, Development and Advice). The foundation's activities show characteristically how people can go forward - step by step- in a development whose aim is more or less anticipated, but whose concrete way of accomplishing it is as yet unknown. The way here is more similar to a series of experiments, searching for the "right answer" rather than the result of a systematic planning exercise.

Marleen now has a project group around her and they consist of a bio-ecological architect, a project manager, an urban planner, a permaculture designer, a specialist in water systems and a specialist in sustainable energy systems. She has found professional partners in the alderman and the city manager, both of Culemborg, who support the project in the local politics and administration. These people all work on an advocacy basis with some people from Culemborg and the future residents - in an intense dialogue of planning charettes where other architects and planners are invited in to comment and give further ideas. In this way, Margrit and Declan Kennedy from Lebensgarten, Steyerberg together with Joachim Eble, Tübingen, the architect of many ecological settlements in Germany, were involved in evaluating the progress, the developing concepts, the preliminary design proposals and the implemental schedules.

Contact:
Culemborg
Marleen Kaptein
Amsterdijk 11a
1071 HR Amsterdam
Netherland

Tel: +31 20 671 17 34
Fax: +31 20 664 43 63

Wilhelmina Terrein

In the Amsterdam borough called Oud-West there is an urban eco-village with quite unusual characteristics. The Wilhelmina hospital was originally built in 1891. In contrast to the surrounding area of densely inhabited and solid rows of apartment buildings, this complex represents a peaceful green oasis. It consists of a number of renovated and converted former hospital buildings, some new buildings as well as carefully designed and planted public green spaces. Thanks to the activities of a local action group, which is responsible for initiating the project, demolition was prevented.

Apart from the flats there are a health centre, a kindergarten, a section of the Film Academy, a cycling club, a futon manufacturer, a workshop making wooden toys and a painter's, a decorator's shop and senior citizens' apartments in this urban eco-village

Ecology played an important part, especially for pavilions 1 and 2, and as a result this part of the Wilhelmina hospital renewal has become a unique area in Amsterdam. It was carried out by a members' working party in co-operation between the borough of Oud-West and a housing association. Ecological renewal included:

Wilhelmina Terrein

- healthy building: low-toxic materials used for pavilions 1 and 2
- energy/heating: use of passive solar energy and solar panels for hot water on south facing roofs, CHP combined generation of electricity and heat
- water: water saving taps, some rainwater collection
- open spaces: members take care of the green spaces themselves, keep small domestic animals, and plant more trees to improve the micro-climate
- traffic: whole complex is mainly car free, parking spaces available on periphery, access only to pedestrians and cyclists, noise barrier provided by dense vegetation alongside main road
- design: renovation, roof gardens, greenhouses, many building façades with vegetation, a renovated shell with connections to all services (gas, electricity, heat, water, sewage) was provided within the old buildings to members by the association to renovate for themselves

The social concept is based on the idea that the residents took over responsibility of renovating the inside of the old hospital buildings, also for preventative health care, children's nursery and play areas. Rents are very moderate because members can implement their own interior design within a renovated building shell. The skills shown by members were some of the determining factors in the choice of environmental measures. The redevelopment of the two pavilions shows how successful active collaboration by people living in the project in urban renewal projects can be. 86 apartments, 24 businesses, including workshops for senior citizens and unemployed. This was an educational process for all those involved. The result for both the housing association and the city of Amsterdam, but especially the borough of Oud-West, was the increasing incorporation of ecological considerations into their work elsewhere.

Wilhelmina Terrein

Contact:
Ytzen Taminga,
Stichting WH Terrein,
c/o Rataplan Architecten,
le Helmerstraat 17H
1054 CX Amsterdam
Netherlands

Tel/Fax: +31 20 683 96 18

Mourne Grange
Northern Ireland
Kilkeel
existing
eco-village

Mourne Grange is a village community of more than 130 people, where mentally and physically disadvantaged adults live and work together with co-workers and their families.

Lying in the foothills of the Mourne Mountains in peaceful rural surroundings, Mourne Grange has a village atmosphere in which everyone knows what is happening and is interested and concerned in the life of the place.

Co-workers in our Camphill centres receive no wages, but the community provides for their individual needs, which can vary from person to person. The basis for this is described by Rudolf Steiner:

"In a community of human beings working together, the well-being of the community will be the greater, the less the individual claims for himself the proceeds of the work he himself has done, i.e. the more of these proceeds he makes over to his fellow workers the more his own requirements are satisfied, not out of his own work done, but out of the work done by others".

Out of this, a way of life can grow in which each member of the community is integrated into a social setting where, in addition to finding the dignity of every human being, he can experience that his contribution is valued, needed and serves the good of the whole community.

Life in the various households is like that of a family, since co-workers and their children, young and old people alike, live together without the restriction of shifts and rotas or payment for work or time given. The farm of about 100 acres, vegetables gardens and orchards, as well

Mourne Grange

as the village store, laundry and bakery, all serve the needs of the community. There are a number of craft workshops where products are made for sale in the community,s craft shop and tea-room, and elsewhere.

The new Village Hall is a centre for the social and cultural life of the community, and regular non-denominational services are held in the chapel.

A busy working life, whether in house, workshop, or on the land, calls on everyone according to individual capabilities.

Evenings, weekends and fixed times during the day offer the opportunity for adult education as well as social and cultural activities, both within and outside the community.

Mourne Grange is a registered charity. Together with Clanabogan Camphill Village Community near Omagh, and Glencraig Camphill Community near Holywood, it is a subsidiary of the Glencraig Camphill Trust and also registered charity, which is responsible not only for capital and its expenditure but also plays an important advisory role in the development of all three Camphill Centres in Nothern Ireland. It receives grants from Government Departments and Agencies. As well as receiving financial and practical help, a community such as Mourne Grange needs to be supported by a wider group of people who share a conviction and awareness of what the disadvantaged person has to offer. The shortfall is met by funds raised by the "Friends of Glencraig Camphill" by the "Mourne Grange Camphill Village Association" and by direct donations and legacies.

Contact:
Mourne Grange Camphill Village Community:
Silke Kindler
Newry Road, Kilkeel
Co. Down, BT34 4EX
Northern Ireland

Tel: +44 16 93 76 22 28

Vallersund Gaard, a Camphill village community, has close connections to the other 6 Norwegian Camphill villages and the 85 Camphill villages and schools all over the world. Co-workers, villagers and some former drug users have transformed a run down nineteenth-century fishing centre into Vallersund Gaard with fishing, a farm, a bakery, a stone workshop, a cafeteria, a little chapel, a wind generator for electricity and interesting water treatment systems.

Women and men who come to Vallersund to get hold of their lives, to work, to study or to visit will soon give in to the irresistible rhythm of the village. They live together, they have punctual meals together, go out to work, relax in privacy, meet to study and to have discussions.

Weekdays, Sundays, holidays, leisure and work, early mornings, late evenings are mostly shared and spent together. In the house where you live with the family of co-workers and their children and with handicapped and other people, retiring to your own room is regarded with the utmost respect for privacy for the individual. Living together can be confronting, because your own self is being reflected by the others constantly. And everybody stimulated by therapy and surrounded by the community will have to meet with their real self.

The Camphill philosophy is based on the conviction that equality in a community is the best breeding ground for the development of the individual. Coming to Vallersund is meeting a wide variety of individuals from many different cultures and walks of life, in a background of breath-taking scenery.

117

Vallersund Gaard

The community of Vallersund Gaard is adjusted to its natural environment - a little below the Polar Circle. It takes time to let personalities manifest themselves fully, in order to allow personal development as well as the formulation of important decisions in peoples lives to take shape. All villagers contribute, give to the community as well as take, receive from it. They work together, each testing their own abilities, and give or receive. Work is in the bakery, in the garden, working with stone, making dolls, working in the stables, on the land, in the shop and in the house. They perform plays, frequently, they have spiritual study meetings, cultural gatherings and celebrate seasonal festivities. Or they attend lessons.

The many nationalities, cultures and views and the exchange in the village (as often playful as deeply serious) help the Vallersund community to cope with personal crises. Crises people have to go through. Crises touch the community deeply, since they show the loneliness can

118

occur in spite of the communal togetherness. But you can share your crisis with the community. And when you come through it the benefits of the crisis work further in the community.
And so it is with laugh-
ter. There are many
laughs and they can be
shared. It is good to see
someones happiness in
achievement.   And
laughter can be shared
while trying and trying
again, during all the
little failings.

All villagers participate in the weekly general meeting. Comings and goings of villagers and visitors are discussed; everybody, using Norwegian as common language, expresses in his own way what plans or critical questions he or she has in mind. When the word has completed the circle of villagers and visitors, it is as if a song has been heard. Outside winter may be making its own windy music when the meeting adjourns and the participants are stomping down the wooden staircase in their heavy boots. In the half light of mid morning, they shuffle through sleet or snow, back to the well heated, cosy houses. Relaxing for a moment someone takes a guitar from a corner of the living room and hums a song. And there is more music. Many bring instruments to Vallersund Gaard, violins, guitars, wooden flutes, or just their voice to lead or join in singing. A glockenspiel may be used during a coffee-break to form an orchestra.

Early in the morning, the small cows are settling comfortably to the familiar hands of an Austrian, a Norwegian or maybe a German villager. Hands that are kept busy through the days. Cleaning stables, moving farming equipment, driving a horse pulling a plough. Hands are shaping rough pieces of stone into beautifully coloured clocks or jewellery in the stone workshop. Next-door a tantalising smell leads to a large bakery, where a group of villagers is baking bread. A cowhand may later be busy

Vallersund Gaard

pulling lines and hooks from the depth of the fjord in the afternoon, hoping for salmon rather than cod. And the man responsible for a reading session with mentally handicapped will try his hand at gardening. Hands will be painting, modelling clay or doing needle work, or painting the wooden walls of the houses in summer. Whatever, the hands are creative instruments, shaping, expressing, achieving.

Focal point of hand activity for everyone is preparing meals, washing the dishes by hand, cleaning the house. All this work is savoured because it is fulfilling life for the villagers. The introduction of telephones from house to house is judged a pity by some, it substitutes walking to talk face to face. Let alone introducing a dish washing machine. Never. It would take away handwork that is a binding factor among the villagers in the houses.

Living in a community, however respectful of the individual, is never easy for young and grown up women and men. Perhaps children are the best at it. They take life as it presents itself. Their Camphill family has almost no limits and is always close. In the six houses and for all the thirty odd inhabitants of Vallersund the meals are the focal points of the community. The most important dish is the conversation. Someone will always start it and everybody joins in. Sometimes language difficulties or speech problems have to be overcome. There are always interesting topics, there is gentle teasing but there are also undercurrents of tension. That is what makes conversation lively. However punctual, the meals are creative, free and relaxed.

Contact:
Vallersund Gaard
Gerrit Overweg
7167 Vallersund
Norway

Tel: +47 72 52 73 00
Fax: +47 72 52 78 95
e-mail: overweg@online.no

Dabrówka   Poland

Lublin
existing
eco-village

Our community has been building up slowly since 1976 and found its home in seven villages in south-eastern Poland near the town of Lublin - so it is not really one eco-village, but a co-operative project of units spread over the countryside. With time the presence of the newcomers was accepted by the local villagers and we have a close relationship based on mutual respect which is very important to us and one of the reasons for being here. After 20 years of existence we are about 100 people in 25 families in our community. The older generation is now in its forties, the youngest in the twenties. All 25 families together inhabit 29 houses.

Each family here makes its own living and every one of us has found a unique way of doing it. A few of us also work in town. We have small gardens which provide us with fruit and vegetables. One family has three goats. Handicraft is an income for quite a few of us. The diversity of items produced here is very wide: sculpture, furniture, totems, clothes made of tissue and leather, patchwork, shoes, tipis, toys, chess, buckwheat pillows, jewellery and more. We also produce drums, which in the meantime are world famous. An important part of our income is building and restoration in the region. We have good experience with ecological building and water treatment. We have also started to regularly plant trees together.

Dabrówka

We play and record music, teach foreign languages and do literary translations. Music workshops are organised regularly in our village for both our countrymen and guests from abroad. All in all, we use our skills in a very creative way.

In 1995, we created the association "For Earth" and members of the association own 40 ha of land. Our most important goal is to implement ecological agriculture. A few years ago a tractor factory gave us a tractor to test. With time we have the opportunity to become more self-sufficient. We hope that through the association we can gain knowledge in organic food production and establish contacts with the producers of healthy food.

We are working towards becoming partners with our local municipality and regional government. The unemployment in our region is high. Our aim is to promote healthy food production in the small farms around us.

The land on which we live is inhabited by many endangered species. We work actively for protecting wildlife habitats. Both our children and ourselves are active in other associations protecting the wildlife.

Contact:
Association For Earth
Nicole Grospierre
Dabrówka 30
21-134 Staroscin
Poland

Tel: +48 83 65 40 91 ex. 360

122

Tamera is a German research project in Portugal, started in spring 1995. It is a site of 134 hectares (330 acres) in the south of Portugal, about 20 km (12 miles) away from the west coast. Kork oaks, citrus, olive groves, brambles and thistles grow here. We have an orchard and a small orange nursery, several lakes and various springs. Tamera, Centre for Human Ecology, is a co-operative of people who work for the future with the intention to build a model for a non-violent culture. Our goal is to build a research settlement where the most important themes of a new, sustainable culture concept are developed. The main themes are:

- spiritual ecology and the community of all beings
- the building of well-functioning communities
- love, sexuality, partnership and children
- the human being in the universe. Mysteries of creation
- nature research and biotope research
- technology for sustainable energy supply (solar and wind), basic research in information technology, resonance technology and the use of free cosmic energy
- the research of spiritual awareness (perception) and dreams
- nutrition research (to increase the ability to perceive finer energies)

Tamera

Our goal is the sustainable supply in the aspects of energy, water, food and medicine and in the aspect of human transformation towards increased ability to love, awareness, good health and planetary thinking. At present, there are about 200 people who take part in the building of Tamera, 15 of whom form the permanent team.

Many of those who work on site are guests who want to participate and help with the project. For the next couple of years, the main emphasis will be on building up the necessary working and living accommodation. The large hall is already in use. Something like a philosophical building group has arisen with changing members whereby crafts and technical know-how are connected with spiritual content.

The goal of the ecological work at Tamera is the creation of a healthy biosphere of people, animals and plants. The healing forces of all living beings can work together when there is no more fear or mistrust between them. Trust is an entree of non-violent ecology. Such an insight has far-reaching consequences. We will have to consider such activities as hunting, fishing, eating meat, etc. We do not have an answer to this question yet, as we are not approaching these answers through a law, but rather through experience and recognition. Our ecological concept includes reducing consumption, a highly developed recycling system, vegetarian food, creating several permaculture experimental stations and to increase nature's self-healing power through planting certain plants or placing art at geomantic cross points.

Most important within the ecological concept of Tamera is a healthy social ecology among people. When the hidden resistance of fear and violence between people have disappeared, then self-healing forces of love, trust and co-operation can unfold. Fear has to disappear first, as fear is the ecological bottleneck of communication among people and with nature. Loving without fear and living without lies, this could be the motto for the Tamera project. But not regarded as a law. Anyone who wants to live and permanently work at this place can purchase his own power spot. The first group are building their cabins close to each other to preserve the natural surroundings. There is no one religious or spiritual commitment, but a communal direction which determines the character of the place. A number of courses and work camps are taking place all over the year, but it is necessary to call us, if you want to visit Tamera. Office time: Monday to Friday 9.00 -12.00 a.m. local time.

Contact:
Tamera
Monte Cerro
7655 Colos
Portugal

Tel: +351 83 633 06
Fax: +351 83 633 74
e-mail: tamera@mail.telepac.pt
web site: www.ecovillages.org/tamera

Ecopolis

Ecopolis was founded in the Siberian taiga, and since the summer of 1994, about 2 thousand people have made their constant residence in about 30 villages and settlements close to the region chosen for the construction of the city of the Sun. The majority of the settlers have families and the average age is 36-37 years. The number of settlers is growing constantly and in the summer it is doubled. Half of the adults have high education and the majority of these, 60%, have technical education. 90% are Russian and there are also settlers of other nationalities: Belorussians, Ukrainians, Kazakhs, Letts, Tatars, Armenians and Jews.

The main eco-settlement with 120 houses has a radial circular design. There are buildings in the centre of the circle for spiritual and cultural activities, workshops for folk and art trades and houses for young people. The one-family farm-steads are situated along 14 radial axes. The maximum conservation of the natural landscape is foreseen in the fields between farmsteads. Temporary buildings provide space for 100 persons in summer and 40 persons in winter.

The building of the Unified Religion Temple is planned separately on the Sukhaja mountain beside the lake of Teberkool. A small settlement consisting of 9 buildings in the Temple zone is also planned. At present, the general layout of the settlement has been drawn up with working drawings of the starting complex, which includes 7 one-family living houses, 1 house for young people and 2 workshops, designed in the traditional Russian wood architectural style.

In the Ecopolis there is no cattle-breeding, no fish-breeding, no meat or milk industry as all the new settlers are strict vegetarians. No alcohol, no narcotics, no smoking. The main foods are fruits, vegetables, nuts, cereals and leguminous plants. In healthcare, natural medicine systems are used for preventive and curative treatment and school medicine is only used in cases of extreme necessity.

Waldorf pedagogics and home teaching will allow the development of the children´s souls and abilities on the base of games and creative work, joy of work in particular. The secondary school with ecological

Ecopolis

and art-aesthetic emphasis began its work in Chememshanka in September 1998.

Unique masters of the folk crafts (about 50) from different places of Russia and other countries are gathering here: there are carpenters and blacksmiths successfully working and forming workshops. There are also sculptors and masters of pottery. Women are busy with weaving, embroidering and other needleworks. Much attention is paid to music, singing and choreography. First class workers of art have come from Moskow and St-Petersburg and can teach all who wishes their art. There exists a church choir (loved by everyone) under Anna Boodko, a former solist of the Bolshoy theatre in Moskow.

The only power used is the energy of wind, sun and water. The settlers restore old agricultural technology, using horse transport since 1997.

Proposals for the use of airship instead of helicopters are being discussed because of the lack of paved roads in the taiga. Other appropriate technologies, like a horse-powered elevator for the building of the temple, are part of our experimental programmes. Especially alluring is the idea of using these and other ecologically means for transporting loads during the construction of the Temple of the Unified Faith in the centre of the Ecopolis. There are wonderful marble beds at the foot of the mountain that have to be raised quite some height. In June 1996, that elevator was made in Moskow and was delivered in August to the mountain Sookhaja. Now it is in work. It is possible to use semi-conductor thermo-generators for electricity going into ordinary stoves. The high scientifical and technical potential of St-Petersburg and other cities and countries can be used also in other fields of engineering to support this wonderful eco-city, beginning near the Teberkool eco-village.

Contact:
Ekopolis
Kuraginskij Raion
Gulaievka
Zharosk, Teberkol

International Light Centre

In northern Russia at the edge of a vast wilderness, we have founded a community at the confluence of the Vazhenka and Muzhala rivers. The soil is rich, the air and rivers are clean and the local people are genuine. Our community is just beginning, a seed newly sprouted, and we invite you to join us to discover our inner potential and our relationship to the earth through shared work and meditation. We educate, bringing out the innate wisdom and creativity in each person, and help people become self-sufficient doing work they love.

Spiritual: Our community is founded on the belief that every act, every thought, every breath is a prayer and a meditation. We seek the divine in everything and everyone, and realise that all inner paths lead to the same goal. In this spirit we meditate together daily and sponsor seminars by teachers from throughout the world.

Healing: Body, mind and heart are inseparably interconnected, the health of each depending on the health of all. This forms the basis of our holistic approach to healing. We promote the study and practice of alternative healing techniques such as herbal medicine, diet, folk remedies, massage and spiritual healing.

Ecology: Recognising the current crisis facing the global environment,
we seek solutions to the devastation, inflicted upon the earth by modern society. We com-
bine scientific knowledge
with the voice of intui-
tion to discover the path
of balance between our-
selves and nature.

Farming: We strive for
self-sufficiency; to grow
what we eat in our gar-
dens, supplemented by
the wild berries and herbs
of the forests and mea-
dows. We dedicate our-
selves to conservation of
the topsoil through exten-
sive composting and per-
maculture farming tech-
niques.

Folklore: We promote the
preservation of the folk
arts, which are rapidly
being lost to the modern
world. These include folk
songs and dances, blacksmithing, woodworking, ceramics, textiles and
village architecture. We also observe var-ious traditional folk holidays.

Children: To safeguard the future, it is our responsibility to educate our
children to live in harmony with each other and with the earth. Each
summer we offer a children's summer camp to teach ecology, gardening, dance, music, art and folk crafts. We invite teachers from
throughout the world to share their skills and experience.

Community spirit is growing - by heart to heart connections - as people
meet through our dance and children's camp, workshops, and building

International Light Centre

projects. We are learning to live and work together by accepting our differences and celebrating our skills and talents.

Currently, we own three wooden houses along the River Vazhenka in the village Grishino. One of them is a historic village house which became our retreat centre and guest house. We will set it on a stable foundation and repair the roof. We also plan to buy and renovate the other half of our farmhouse.

In the future, we will build a large community house with additional guest rooms, a common kitchen, and a meeting hall for workshops. Eventually, we hope to buy approximately forty acres of meadow lands atop a hill overlooking the village where the soil is fertile and the views are breathtaking. This is where we will build our sanctuary.

We appreciate your support of love, prayers and generous donations to our non-profit foundation. Checks can now be made payable to Grishino Foundation and sent to our contacts.

Contacts:
Vasudeva Kirbiatiev
Basseinaya ul. 59-106
St. Petersburg 196135
Russia

Tel: +7 812 29 44 189
Fax: +7 812 11 35 896
email: Grishino@Dance.spb.su

or

Diana Lee Crow
2888 Bluff St. #493
Boulder, CO 80301,
USA

Tel: +1 303 65 21 627
email: DianaCrow@aol.com

Since 1993, Kitezh has functioned as a non-government, non-profit home and school for orphaned Russian children in a community of foster families who live together on a large piece of land in a rural area 300 km south of Moscow in the Kaluga region. The nearest town is Baryatino. Their system of fostering and educating children has proved to be a real alternative to the state system of orphanages and child-care institutions. Education is the main focus at Kitezh.

Kitezhans aim to live in harmony with nature, in an ecologically a-ware, natural life style, within a village community. They believe that by serving others, they will serve themselves. At present 20 permanent residents live at Kitezh with 30 children, some adopted, others their own. In the summer months, many volunteers and students come to Kitezh to help with building, working in the gardens, on the farm and with the children.

Kitezh is also a wide circle of intellectuals concerned with consolidating their efforts to bring about the changes needed in Russian society today; in economic, social, political, environmental and educational spheres. Several highly educated people - artists, poets, writers and journalists, scientists and scholars - are involved with Kitezh and find it a receptive environment to share their knowledge. Some come to offer special courses and programmes. For them, Kitezh provides a vast field for new experiments in education, in cordial surroundings and with sensitive children who are eager to learn from them.

Kitezh

Kitezh is a new way of looking at life: it is a living, working community, a spiritual movement, and a functioning organisation of people who believe that people in Russia and the rest of the world can build their lives on the principles of harmony, peace and love. It is a fascinating form of eco-village community living, one of its kind in Russia.

The lifestyle at Kitezh is simple. The families live in traditional wooden houses with outside toilets and no running water. They eat simply, mostly home-grown vegetables, dairy products, honey and wild mushrooms. The people are warm, open-hearted and about half speak English. Visitors are always welcome, for just a few days or several weeks or months. Allow a day for travelling between Moscow and Kitezh.

Ecologia Trust, Scotland has worked in partnership with Kitezh since its beginning, supporting this enterprise in many ways, with visitors, exchange groups and raising funds for the development of Kitezh.

In 1996 a youth group from the Findhorn Foundation, Scotland, spent 3 weeks at Kitezh and our children visited Scotland in 1997. Every summer a group of young Germans come to work as volunteers at Kitezh, and several foreign student volunteers have spent one or two months teaching English to the children, building and working in the gardens. They all have received a unique and wonderful experience. Visitors live with one of the families and take part in the daily working life and community celebrations.

First time visitors will be met in Moscow and brought by car to Kitezh, a 4 or 5 hour journey depending on road conditions. There is also a daily public bus from Moscow to Baryatino which takes 7-8 hours. We

need to know well ahead of time
when and where you will arrive
and for how long you will stay.
A Summer School for Foreign
Students take place each July
and August. They will live in a
camp with other students from
all over Russia and take part in
a rich cultural programme
including Modern Russian His-

tory, Language, Literature, Religion and Culture. For our Volunteers
Program, School Leavers GAP Year and the Summer School for Foreign Students, contact Ecologia Trust (e-mail below) in Scotland who
will help you organise your travel and visa to visit Kitezh. Costs will
be supplied on request.

A video of Kitezh, filmed in winter '97, in English, is available from
Ecologia Trust for £20 sterling or U$35.

Contact:
Findhorn Foundation
Liza Hollingshead
The Park, Forres
IV36 OTZ Morayshire
Scotland

Tel/Fax: +44 13 09 69 09 95
e-mail: ecoliza@rmplc.co.uk

or
Dimitry Morosov
Kitezh, Kaluzhaskaya oblast
Baryatino rayon
249650 Russia

Tel: +7 84 54 23 224
e-mail: kitezh@kaluga.ru
web site: www.ecovillages.org/russia/kitezh

Nevo Ecoville

Nevo Ecoville is one of the original two Russian eco-villages in the GEN seed group. It is situated adjacent to the village of Reuskula, not far from the town of Sortavala, Republic of Karelia. It is on the northern coast of the Ladoga lake and 300km north of the city of St. Petersburg. The site has 26 hectares of food production, 10 hectares set aside for housing and 1,5 hectares for production facilities. At present the initiating team includes 12 persons from the age of 28 to 70, all of high

educational level. There are architects (3), geographers (2), technical engineers (2), foresters (2), teachers (2) and an agronomist.

The idea of the "Nevo Ecoville" was set up in 1987. The construction work started in 1994. The Centre for Ecological Initiatives "Nevo Ecoville" was registered as a public association in 1995.

We took as motto Seneka's statement "To live happily and to live according to nature is the same ". It is essential that a new environment-minding philosophy emerge which alone can assure integrity and vitality of the entire system, in order to assure survival, to encourage exercise of the creative and spiritual potential of human beings and to open new qualitative horizons for the development of the biosphere.

Goal: to set up an environmental production, research and education centre on the northern coast of Ladoga lake.

Objectives:
- to construct a compact residential community following the principles of environmentally clean technologies and functional self-sufficiency
- to set-up a research station and testing grounds for the studies and restoration of traditional techniques and for the development and testing of new environmentally safe life-supporting technologies
- to found a School of Ecology in order to assist in shaping ecological and environmental oriented thinking
- to set up an organisation for environmental monitoring, providing expert and consulting services in the field of ecology
- to study bioenergetics and information capabilities for the correction of critical environmental situations due to anthropogenic effects
- to participate in the global environmental movement, especially in the organisation of various forms of ecological tourism
- to participate actively in the organisation and activities of the Ladoga Skerries National Park
- to assist in shaping public opinion through the mass media on the need to preserve and use responsibly the unique natural and cultural system of the Ladoga coast

The entire package of the Centre's production facilities and services is planned to be used as its research division which will also offer a test ground for other institutes, manufacturers and agencies. This division is expected to have:
- Laboratory for Environmentally Safe Technologies
- Laboratory for Comprehensive Environmental Analysis
- Laboratory for Energy Information Exchange
- Environmental Research Data Bank

Nevo Ecoville

The Ecology School will be an inherent element of a broad environmental education system, acting both as a distinct entity and a structural component of this system - through moral, cultural, environment-oriented ecological education and practical training.

To assure spiritual, social, cultural and household needs, the residential complex is intended to be a working model of an environmentally clean self-sufficient settlement, using environmentally safe technologies for everyday requirements. Already constructed is new house for 2 families with some guest rooms, a bath-house, a small summer house, vegetable storage cellars and a chicken house. An electric line and a road has been constructed to the centre of the site. Planned production facilities assuring economic independence, are construction, farming, reforestation and landscaping, tourism and commerce. A construction firm and a horticulture business are functioning already.

contact:
Nevo Ecoville
Ivan S. Goncharov
Central Post Office, General Delivery
Ryuskula Village
186750 Karelia Republic
Russia

Fax: +7 812 113 58 96
e-mail: nevo@onego.ru
or   vshestak@neva.spb.ru

Rysovo **Russia**

Novgorod

existing

eco-village

Rysovo is one of the original two Russian eco-villages in the GEN seed group. Rysovo is being constructed on 166 hectares of land in the Novgorod region, south of St.Petersburg. The land is on the site of a village which was abandoned in 1945, partly due to natural urban drift and partly due to the Soviet policy of urbanisation. There is no electricity, no telephone and access to the nearest village by road is difficult for most vehicles. One wooden house is left from pre-war years.

Due to the lack of accommodation on the site, log cabins are being built using local timber. Log cabins are cool in summer and warm in winter, the gaps in the walls being filled with clay. Ironically, they were always built by the poor, the wealthier preferring stone, which meant that the poor were at least warmer in the harsh Russian winter. It is very common in Russia to live and work during winter in a city and return to one's village in summer - and Rysovo is no exception. There is a winter population of 5 which swells dramatically during summer with outside helpers. It is planned to build up the village for 20-25 families.

In order to build the project, a portable sawmill was bought with assistance from Gaia Trust, Denmark. The sawmill is, of course, used not just for Rysovo, but also does work for local neighbouring villages. Lebensgarten, Germany, assisted Rysovo some years back in inviting their Russian colleagues to learn mud-building techniques in Northern Germany and donated the monies for the equipment which the participants took back with them.

137

Rysovo

On the site can be found different kinds of animals at differnet times of the year: elk, wolf, hare, boar, fox, water-fowl and hog game and a big colony of beavers. There are many mosquitoes in summer. The extreme rural nature of Rysovo can be seen where haymaking is a labour intensive job from start to finish, using no machinery whatsoever. Small scale farming and berry picking are the mainstays of the village which has purposely chosen to start up from scratch, using old methods and crafts.

Apart from the residential areas which will be dotted all over the site, five specific zones are planned in this eco-village:
- common zone (place for meeting, post-boxes, chapel, parking place, fire equipment, anbulence and bus stop, etc.)
- scientific zone (school, library, information centre, art studio, etc.)
- economic (garage, mechanical shop, wood-processing shop, food storage, food processing and bakery, farm shop, cold storage, visitors accomodation, canteen, etc.)
- agricultural zone (cultivated land, hay-making places, pastures, etc.)
- resting places (splaces for games, gardens, etc.). The common house has been designed by the young Russian-American architect David Been in 1996, but funding is still not available.
It will include:
  - rooms for 3-4 tempoary visitors (like hotel)
  - big room for meetings, workshops (like conference hall)
  - kitchen and dining room
  - room for library, reading room, information desk
  - administrative office
  - place for washing, storing water, showers, toilets, laundry and drying
  - place for drying mushrooms, berries, herbs and cold storage
  - joinerer and carpenter workshop

138

A model as visualized by *Irena Olegovna*

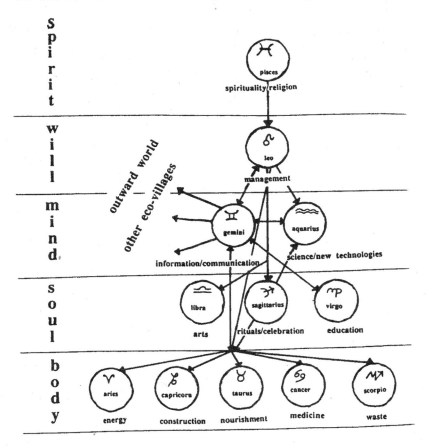

Scheme

Eco-village as an alive organism, as a mikrocosm

Russia
Novgorod
existing
eco-village

Rysovo

There is a summer camp each year where visitors from the West, mostly Scandinavia and other Russian regions, come to help Rysovians with construction work. The tents and catering facilities are Russian army surplus and are used outside of the summer camp season as tempoarary dwellings for helpers, who live in cities normally, to participate in building this community. There are some complications with projects of this nature, communication being the most obvious, usually done through people travelling to and from the St. Petersburg Eco-village Information office, which was the communication centre and one of GEN's first network nodes in Eastern Europe until June 1997.

Contact:
Rysovo Village
P.O.Yakovishchy,
Moshenskoy District
17443 Novgorod Region
Russia

Tel: +7 812 513 30 19
         Andrej O. Leontiev
Fax: +7 812 235 71 83

140

We are an international community and developing eco-village of about 350 people living, studying and working together in the north-east of Scotland. The community was founded in 1962 by Eileen Caddy, Peter Caddy and Dorothy Maclean in a caravan park a mile from the seaside village of Findhorn. First known for our work with plants and nature, we have since become a centre for spiritual and holistic education as well. While we have no formal doctrine or creed, we honour and recognise all the major world religions, believing that there are many paths to God. Our focus is on learning to bring spiritual principles into our daily lives through our work, the way we relate to each other, and how we express our caring and concern for the Earth.

The Findhorn Foundation runs an educational centre and offers a wide variety of courses in such fields as personal and spiritual growth, conflict resolution, gardening, meditation, leadership, community living,

and the arts. The community is also actively engaged in environmental projects, including the construction of innovative ecological housing, the use of renewable energy systems and community-based recycling schemes; Trees for Life, a conservation charity dedicated to the regeneration and restoration of the Caledonian Forest. There are a number of organisations and businesses that are either part of, or are associated with, the Findhorn Bay Community: Findhorn Bay Caravan Park, Gnosis, Findhorn Press, the Pottery, Healthworks and others.

Motivated by ideas generated at the Planetary Village conference held here in 1982, the Findhorn Community spent the next six years planning and preparing for the transformation into an ecological village. As we define it, an eco-village is a human settlement that is sustainable ecologically, economically, culturally and spiritually; that expresses our

Findhorn Bay Community

essential relationship and connection to spirit and nature through its forms and structures. Sustainability is the ability of an ecosystem, a community or a person to maintain itself over the long term, without depleting or damaging any essential functions.

Early in the community's history there was a collective realisation that a working partnership and tangible sense of connection and co-operation with Nature was possible. In fact, it is not just possible, but increasingly essential in our human endeavours in the physical world that we recognise the needs of nature and the natural systems, and honour these as we seek to meet our human needs.

Starting in an ageing caravan park with 120 caravans and mobile homes, arguably the worst possible dwellings imaginable in ecological terms, we have gradually begun the process of replacement. In our ecological building programme, we have built 16 dwellings to high ecological standards with a unique breathing wall construction system. In terms of renewable energy, we operate a wind turbine and manufacture solar panels. We have increased our production and distribution of organic food and instituted a community health care plan that is affordable and offers a wide range of complementary practitioners.

An ‚eco-village' is much more than just a collection of energy efficient homes with the latest in green gadgets, from solar panels to CFC-free fridges. The need to create a truly ‚ecological' and sustainable lifestyle encompasses far more than the physical or environmental issues of humanity, though it includes these. Our social, cultural and political systems must reflect our human needs for community, creativity, education, growth and self-expression. Our collective impact on the planet

will reflect our own inner state. When we are in balance with ourselves
we can act from a place of wholeness that respects and honours all life.
We have started to develop a new form of commerce that is based on
supporting the long term needs of humans and nature, diversifying our
economy to include a range of fledgling businesses and a LETS system
of alternative economic exchange.

Contact:
Findhorn Foundation
The Park
Findhorn,
Forres IV36 OTZ
Scotland

Tel: +44 1309690311
e-mail: vcentre@findhorn.org
web site: www.gaia.org

Earth Sanctuary

The current Project was started during the Harmonic Convergence in 1987. The land covers 150 ha of wild Catalan mountain, 150 km, South of Barcelona.

There are 15 adult and 4 children (aged 10-19). We run our own school, the "Little Forest", which is connected to Clonlara - Home schooling Programme, Michigan, U.S.A. Children are always very welcome.

Our economic system is based on donations, rents and workshops: Transpersonal counselling, Art-Therapy, and crafts such as Raku pottery. Through time, we have evolved our own technique for group encounters, which is very close to Arnold Mindell,s "Process-oriented Psychology". Our main focus include: deep ecology (Gaia consciousness), creation spirituality and group processes (based on humanistic and transpersonal psychology), gender-peace and women's spirituality. The group started as a Poona- like community of 80 people in 1981, and evolved towards a more nature-centred approach through time, a change clearly focused in the 1987 Harmonic Convergence. At that point Shakti started to work with the community as a transpersonal psychotherapist.

Earth Sanctuary

We are initiated as Sannyasins and we think that life is a Sacred Journey. Our relationships tend to be intense, as we utilise them as a tool for personal transformation. Our common aim is to create a sanctuary for trees, animals, and... humans!... as a political statement for the Millennium. The concrete aim is to create a Garden of Eden (or Avalon).

At this point of our development as a community, we are not too interested in the new technologies, though this may happen soon. We are more centred in the elaboration of techniques for conflict resolution, as this seems a priority for the human race if we are to reach the Millennium at all!... In particular, we are dedicated to Gender peace. The war between sexes is the mother of all wars, and this is our main preoccupation for our children. Since 1987, we have elaborated techniques to address this problem squarely, and we even have reached certain solutions, which we would be happy to offer.

Contact:
The Earth Sanctuary Project
Shakti Genaine
Apdo 17
43460 Alcover
Spain

Lakabe

Lakabe is situated in a beautiful valley about 50 km from the town of Pamplona. Over the last 10 years the regional government have had plans to build a hydroelectric power plant in the valley. The commune of Lakabe occupied an abandoned village in 1980 with the aim to make it an alternative village. The commune is based on antiauthoritary and non-violence principles.

One of the strong points on the programme of the commune is self sufficiency with food and energy and it has been achieved within the potentials of this place. All electricity comes from a windmill and a gas powered generator (a bigger windmill is planned). The gardens are very big and are the main food source of Lakabe.

At one point the population reached 50 person children included. Today there are 12 adults and 15 children in Lakabe. Together they occupy 7 houses. The children have their own playground, with a small football yard. The economy is common and personal necessities are covered by the commune. The small businesses and workshops are: pottery, carpentry and wool spinning. Twice a week the commune bakes bread and brings it to their distributor in the nearby town of Pamplona.

A bigger bakery has recently been build to meet the food production regulations

The commune has a guest house and the maximum guest capacity is of 20-25 people. The old church in the village is now used for seminars or as a gathering space.

Contact:
Lakabe
Valle de Arce
31438 Nafarroa-Euskadi
Spain

Tel/Fax: +34 948 39 20 02

Spain
Facinas
eco-village
initiative

Arte Elemental

The Galeria Arte Elemental community is situated in the hills not far from a village in the neighbourhood of Cadiz and its beaches. At present, we are 13 residents with 10 further external members. This is a cultural meeting-place and we are promoting art that serves the community, especially music and dance, in its function as a healing force. We have an art and craft gallery, a natural food kitchen and a small shop selling natural food products and crafts. We organise art, craft and personal development workshops. In our philosophy, art, health and natural nutrition form a unity.

We have a permaculture-garden, a herbs and pesto production with roughly 30% of our food self-sufficiency. We recycle our water for irrigation purposes and have compost toilets. Our buildings are hand crafted with natural materials. We generate 100% of our electricity and use almost only renewable energy resources, with about 80% of self-reliance in all our energy uses.

Plans are also underway for the construction of a dance studio and more accommodation for visiting groups with some retreat bungalows in the forest behind the project. Management is on a rotational basis in order to avoid the pitfalls of a hierarchical structure. We have weekly sharing meetings and a lot of collective work. Decisions are made on a consensus basis.

Our centre needs committed earth-repairers, adventurers and pioneers, woofers and volunteers, ready for positive action.

Contact:
Associacion Arte Elemental
Luciano Furcas
Calle Merced 33
11391 Facinas
Spain

Tel: +34 56 23 64 88
Fax: +34 56 68 20 13
e-mail: c.tarifa@arrakis.es

Linden co-operative economic association is made up of a dozen families who are working together to create an "alternative" lifestyle - an
adventure which started in 1990. We have planned and are building an
eco-village in Ubbhult which is located 40 km SE of Gothenburg. It is
named Aspekullen (Aspen Hill) after the original name for the place.

Ubbhult, a village with around 1000 inhabitants has origins as a forestry and farming district dating back to the 14th. century. Today there
is a school, day nursery, clothes shop, hairdresser, builders merchants,
farms and forestry, etc. The surrounding countryside is rich and varied
in a way typical for this part of Sweden, with lakes, tarns, bogs, conife-
rous and deciduous forest, hills and valleys, arable and grazing land
which contribute to a rich natural flora and fauna.

Aspekullen is as much a social project as actual physical buildings.
The early co-operative stages have laid the basis for relationships and
ways of working together which will develop in our community as it
matures. Our aim has been to seek knowledge and understanding of
both ecological and social complexes and to plan, build and administer
Aspekullen ourselves as far as possible.

Aspekullen

Self-contained local ecological systems are a corner stone of ecological thinking. At Aspekullen, this will be achieved through co-operation with a local farmer who will supply us with food and return our waste to the land. The farm, Gunnagard, has been owned and managed by the Niklason family since 1981. From the outset, they have avoided the use of pesticides and artificial fertilisers according to standards set by KRAV (Sweden's supervisory group for approving organic food production). Gunnagard currently produces organic vegetables, grain (flour, etc.) milk and meat of the highest quality.

Aspekullen offers us the opportunity to fulfill our vision of collective living in a spirit of accepting environmental limitations and of the good life. The community building in the centre of the village will play a central roll in this, and will include shared workshops which can be used for handicrafts, etc., by anyone who needs such facilities. It is important that there is space available for both planned and spontaneous meetings and work.

Planning of the project has been carried out by the village members and all decisions are taken on a consensus basis. Expertise is brought in from outside when the need arises. Every family owns their own building plot and is responsible for the construction of their own house. We have good contacts with local craftsmen. Other land, shared facilities, community buildings and others are owned jointly through our co-operative economic association. Self-building and experimentation are encouraged.

There is space in the village for 12 individual family houses, four rented flats, a community building (meeting room, course centre, workshops) and commercial buildings (offices, handicrafts, trading). The building with the four flats, which is owned by the farm, was built in 1997 and one of the other houses is currently under construction. Construction of several more houses will begin in Summer 1998.

The buildings will be constructed from materials which are environmentally sound and which pose no health risk to people, e.g. timber, bricks, clay, earth, straw and recycled materials. Clean water is pumped from an existing well. Waste water is separated in each house. Urine is led to collecting tanks and used by the farmer as a nitrogen fertiliser for grain crops. The dry faeces are composted into a soil conditioner for the flower beds. Each house will have a system for grey water purification in its own greenhouse. Low energy equipment, e.g. earth cooled pantries instead of refrigerators, will be used. Houses will be positioned and planned to take advantage of natural light and passive solar heating and will have supplementary heat with firewood from the forest.

The building plots at Aspekullen are „ready-to-build". By this we mean that outline planning permission has been obtained governing how and where we can build. Each plot has running water, urine drains, electricity and telephone services in place. All that is left is to apply for detailed planning permission and start building. There are still a couple of plots for sale.

Part of the finance for the project has been provided by a member-owned bank, JAK (Earth, Work, Capital), which works for an interest free society. We have also started our own local economic system (based on LETS) and printed our own „bank notes" in the local currency which is called „rydies". We hope this will stimulate people to both offer and ask for help, even in areas not usually valued highly, e.g. baby sitting, cooking, bread making. The farm also uses „rydies" to exchange food for labour.

We did the work involved in drawing up the area plan ourselves. This governs what and how much we can build and has been approved by the local authority. The preparatory administrative work has taken a

151

Aspekullen

considerable amount of our spare time, but has at the same time given us control over the place we have chosen to live and has saved us a lot of money.

The price of each plot is based on the total costs incurred by the project divided by the number of plots. The current price of a building plot at Aspekullen is around SEK 170,000, which includes shared land and buildings. Additional costs include those for registration of title, taxes, connection of electricity and phone services, individual grey water purification facilities, planning permission and, of course the cost of the house. The size of these costs depend on the complexity of the solutions chosen and how much work you are able to do yourself.

The majority of us who intend to build and live at Aspekullen have already moved out to the Ubbhult area. We meet up for various activities, everything from meetings of the association and work days to our „cultural living room" meetings. Several members are also active in local cultural, sporting and political activities. The village has a real need for a place in which to hold training and courses in ecology, building, handicrafts, etc. We hope that the community building will be such a meeting place. Levels of interest in cultivation, animal husbandry and self sufficiency varies considerably. It was, therefore, regarded as important to be able to have one´s own gardens, the chance to rent land for cultivation and, furthermore, co-operate with local farmers. Some of us are also very interested in permaculture design and will at least try to design our own gardens in that direction.

Contact:
Aspekullen Eco-village
Stefan Wallner
Ryde Backe, Ubbhult
430 64 Hällingsjö
Sweden

Tel: +46 301 431 25
e-mail: wallner@arch.chalmers.se

The ecovillage Smeden, a co-housing association, is situated just four kilometres south of the city centre of Jönköping in an area that once was the small church village of Ljungarum – today an integrated part of the modern city, close to the motor way E4. The village is build according to ecological principles and consists of 24 apartments in semi-detached houses with a common village house in addition. The sizes of the apartments vary between 81 and 137 m². Established in the years of 1993-1995.

The initiative of building an ecovillage was originally a political issue of the city council of Jönköping in 1988. By the establishment of an Ecovillage Society in 1990, interested citizens themselves had the opportunity to work for the realisation of the project and to take part in the planning and formation of the village and houses. The participation of the future inhabitants was possible due to a long range co-operation with the architects (Arkitektrådet AB) and the building company (Mjöbäcks Entreprenad AB).

Smeden is located on former farmland, at the edge of a small forest, now a local area of nature preservation. The orientation of the houses is sun facing with the forest at the back (north), thus getting lots of sun radiation on the solar collectors integrated in the roofs and also heat from passive solar power through the triple glazed windows. The fronts

153

Smeden

of the houses are large in-glassed porches – good buffers between in-side and the small gardens outside – with clay floor tiles to store the heat from the sun. The backs of the houses have storage rooms attached to the facade and only one large window. The red wooden houses are well insulated, have few walls without shelter and are build with sound materials. The heating system consists of under-floor hot water pipes heated from solar collectors, and an electric heater in the accumulating water tank. Some apartments have as compliment a tile stove with con-nection to the tank.

Each household has a garden allotment of 200 m² to grow vegetables. Organic household waste is composted and used as fertiliser.

Smeden has its own water supply - a deeply drilled well. The water is treated in an air filter to get rid of iron and make it less hard. The vil-lage also has its own waste water treatment plant for the grey water and flush- water from the toilets. The toilets used in Smeden are water flus-hed and urine-separating. Each apartment has worm compost in a small basement room, where the faeces and paper from the toilets are com-posted after the flush- water is separated. The composted material is dug down in the vegetable gardens to fertilise rhubarbs and berry bushes, etc.

The treated waste water is lead to an artificial pond and stream and continues to a small wetland before it reaches the natural stream that passes the village and later on ends up in a lake. The urine is collected in two common containers, dug down deeply in the ground. The urine and the sludge from the sewage plant are fetched and used by farmers as fertilisers on farmland nearby the village.

All maintenance of the buildings and technical systems are managed by the village inhabitants themselves within the regime of the Co-housing Association. The work is organised in groups of four families, which take turns every fortnight. There are also different working groups for different subjects. Common meetings and parties are held in the village house, which also can be used for hobbies and children's day-care.

The ecovillage is of interest to many different kinds of visitors, and visitors are received and guided by appointment. Lecturing on the eco-village is possible as well.

Contact:
Pia Larsson
Smeden
Korgebovägen 67
553 08 Jönköping
Sweden

e-mail: hellman.larsson@swipnet.se

Tuggelite

Nestling in the Skäre hills a few kilometres north of Karlstad lies Tuggelite - the name means "a little bite". Karlstad is a major provincial town on the edge of the great Lake Vänern in the centre of Sweden and most of the residents of Tuggelite work there as doctors, dentists, teachers or librarians. Fully operational since 1984, Tuggelite ranks as Sweden´s oldest "ecological village". Their beautiful and largely unspoilt countryside is dear to the hearts of most Swedes, and as various threats to its survival were recognised environmental groups sprang up round the country. Initially many of these were protest groups, especially anti-nuclear, which was quite respectable under a strongly Socialist regime. Gradually the focus changed towards more "green" issues and people began looking into ways of conserving natural resources and living more economically in terms of energy consumption and waste creation.

In Sweden building regulations are immensely complex and over-bureaucratised, making it extremely difficult to get private schemes accepted. Several projects are foundering on the rocks of red tape and excessive professional meddling.

This was not the experience of Tuggelite, but that was because of very detailed planning in the first place. The financial and legal aspects had to take precedence over idealistic considerations, although the group never lost sight of their main objectives: an energy-saving environmentally friendly community where people could live together in a mutually supportive way. Tuggelite´s residents claim that they all shared the responsibility and that decisions were taken democratically. Many could help in lobbying, for example, and all could help with manual labour once the stage of laying foundations was reached. In the end the cost of building Tuggelite, in spite of the extra-thickly insulated walls and concrete frame, plus additional features such as greenhouses and porches, compared favourably with conventional building of a similar size. The subsequent running costs of Tuggelite are considerably lower; up to a third less than equivalent buildings of a conventional design.

In a community like this everyone has to be very tolerant. We have learned to listen to each other and to be patient. Of course we have differences of opinion: some would like to see fewer cars in Tuggelite but other people feel that private cars are still necessary. A community vehicle could re-place several private cars here, or else perhaps one car could be shared between families. We are making progress towards group purchase of food. A number of families have a joint arrangement with a local farmer who leaves us fresh unpasteurised milk at the gate, and another farmer provides us with a whole lamb in the slaughtering season.

One growth point in Tuggelite just now is the cultivation of a kitchen garden. Outside the houses we have marked out an area for vegetables; a communal plot which is looked after by ten families, and additional individual plots. This is in addition to the fruits and vegetables we grow in our greenhouses. Produce from these gardens is stored in under-ground earth cellars we built. Unfortunately the soil here is poor, and so we have not had wonderful results with our home-grown vege-tables; only with potatoes and onions. What we cannot grow we try to buy as a co-operative. We also buy all our cleaning products this way.

The parents who are taking maternity or paternity leave to eat together with their children, twice a week, and another group of adults eat an evening meal regularly together, without the children. It is up to each household how much they share social activities - with no pressure being brought on anyone to join in. Then again as our children grow into teenagers we enter a different phase and it is quite possible that we will have more opportunity for socialising in the next few years.

The effect of living in Tuggelite on the older children has been very positive. They appreciate the security the community gives them. They readily help to organise the programme on a "work day", adding their own suggestions. A few years ago they asked for a gymnastic group. There is a strong bond between the children here, who have all grown up together. When the little ones start school, for instance, they find it quite easy to settle in, partly because they have been used to a wide age-range of children around them, but also because the older Tugge-lite children already at the school take special care of them.

It is important that we all share in the maintenance and development of Tuggelite´s community life. We started the practice of monthly

Tuggelite

"village meetings" right from the beginning. We ask for suggestions and ideas beforehand, and sometimes an individual or a group may introduce a topic, but generally the proceedings are very democratic.

Another very important factor in the social organisation of Tuggelite is the work team. We decided that no one was to be employed to clean, garden, cook, or indeed administrate. The adult residents are divided up into five teams who are responsible, in rotation, for the communal tasks. Since we have taken on joint responsibility for cleaning the community centre which includes the laundry room, the kitchen, sauna and the boiler room (the boiler room has to be dealt with every day) besides the main room, there is quite a lot of work involved. Then there is the outside area which we all own and look after together. "Work days" are like mini-work camps when we all get together to do the jobs that have to be done, like clearing up the communal areas outside, gardening, snow-shovelling, etc. We arrange them as often as the need arises, mainly in spring or autumn. Working together is an effective way of looking after the social fabric. This is currently in good repair, to judge from the composition of the community. Of the original sixteen households fourteen were still in residence eight years later. Not a bad record for an experimental community.

We are not all that different from everyone else, it is important not to be too radical too quickly. For one thing children cannot cope easily with being too different from everyone else. Our children go to ordinary local schools and everyone knows where they live. Children do not want to be labelled as "odd" all their school lives, but they can begin to influence others gradually towards a more ecologically sound way of life.

Contact:
Tuggelite
Helena Hultkrantz
Tuggelitevägen 15A
65350 Karlstad
Sweden

Tel: +46 54 53 19 87

158

Underststenshöjden

The first idea came in 1989 from an architectural student. She later became one of the initiators of the project. Now Understenshöjden has 44 homes in 14 one to two storey buildings, placed in four "gardens" and in addition a common house. Homes are between 58 and 155 m², each with its own design. This urban eco-village, only 15 minutes from downtown Stockholm, has developed from a housing project to a social unit of a fairy-tale village character.

The houses are built on pillars for minimum impact on the surrounding environment. The exteriors of the buildings have been coated with ferrous sulphate to quickly weather the wood naturally and beautifully. From the beginning the residents dictated the design, prioritizing: attractive windows, a ceiling height of 2.7 metres, wooden flooring, terra-cotta roofing tiles, floor-plan flexibility, healthy materials, biological water treatment, low-impact construction and 7.5 m² of roof-mounted solar panels on each house. Residents were given the option of buying their houses at one of the following three levels of completion: 1. framed and covered; 2. framed and covered with floors and walls, and 3. turn-key.

Lowering energy consumption was another priority, so apart from the solar panels, air cir-

Understenshöjden

culation by natural convection with intake, vents placed above heating radiators were installed and air exhaust through pipes in kitchens and bathrooms. Toilets were specially constructed to separate solid and liquid wastes - to save water for flushing. The separate urine is stored in two tanks and used as fertiliser in farms outside Stockholm.

Collectively purchasing of organically grown foods creates a city-farm link. Composting, recycling and re-use of all household wastes are aimed at - but not altogether achieved. One room was even built for leaving items that might be practical for other families to re-use.

Contact:
Mia Torpe or Robert af Wetterstedt
Understensvägen 113
Björkhagen
Stockholm
Sweden

or

HSB Stockholm,
112 84 Stockholm,
Sweden

Tel: +46 87 85 30 00
Fax: +46 87 85 32 10

Ces is a small village in the southern Swiss Alps. It is situated on a wild wide plain on 1450 m., high above the Leventina Valley, one of the main traffic connections between Northern and Southern Europe. The village has about 25 houses and stables, some of them in ruins, others already rebuilt. As there is no road leading to Ces, the only way to reach this spot is by walking up the mountain. This takes about two hours, depending on your physical condition.

In the early 70's, some young people discovered Ces as an almost abandoned place. They began to reconstruct houses, started their first garden experiences and got into farming work. To provide these activities with a legal base, the „Foundation for the Renewal of Ces" was found-

ed. Today the „Fondazione" owns one third of the Ces buildings, including five houses, some gardens and plenty of agricultural land. In the summertime there are up to fifty and more persons living in Ces, together with the core group of 5 to 8 persons. This core group keeps the place going in the wintertime. The activities of the Ces community do not follow a special political or spiritual ideology beyond a strong relation to nature and ecology, as well as to community life and social autonomy.

Ces is a remote place, but not isolated: The project aims to have some influence on the „outer world" and demonstrate alternative lifestyles. As we often get visitors from many nations, we are supplied with plenty of new inspiration.

The main working season is from June to September, with a peak in June / July due to the hay gathering work. Our different work branches are: Gardening, agriculture, constructing work, wood chopping and keeping contact with our visitors in the guest house. As we do not use many machines, some of the work is physically strenuous. Working time may be irregular, depending on weather conditions, but takes about eight hours a day. We expect from all participants some efforts in the daily cooking and house work. Officially this is seen as holidays or doing voluntary work.

Usually we offer living and sleeping facilities in one or two of our houses. As we are sleeping in common sleeping rooms with two to ten beds, there is not much privacy inside the houses. Although we built our own small hydro power plant, we decided not to lead electricity wires into every house. Our life is simple: We're cooking on a wood fire stove, and discussions and games are shared by candle light. Organic food is partly produced in our own gardens, partly provided by other suppliers. Although we are not all strictly vegetarians, we do not eat much meat.

The local language is Italian. The members of the „Fondazione" and most of our guests usually speak Swiss German, but some of us are also able to speak English, Italian, French, Dutch or Spanish.

For full time work, we normally provide free food and accommodation. But we appreciate contributions to these costs. For part time work, visitors pay for the food (about CHF 12 a day); just for holidays, CHF 10 in addition for accommodation. We can not pay travelling fee or any other contributions. Please, ensure your accident insurance includes incidents in Switzerland. Please, bring warm clothes and good protection against rain (we do have some Wellingtons), good, strong shoes, a good sleeping bag and a torch. No dogs or other animals.

We invite you to share our community life for one or two weeks. Extension is possible if you fit in. Please, contact us before you arrive to ensure that there is space. To get there: by train from the North: Coming from Basel or Zürich, passing Arth-Goldau and the Gotthard tunnel, leaving the train at Airolo or Faido. From there take a PTT-Bus to Lavorgo. By train from the South: Coming from Milano, Chiasso, Lugano or Locarno, leaving the train at Bellinzona or Biasca. From there take a PTT-Bus to Lavorgo. In Lavorgo take a smaller PTT-Bus to Chironico-Posta. From there you have to walk up the hill, following the yellow signs marked „Ces".

Contact:
Ces
6747 Chironico
Switzerland

Tel: +41 91 865 14 14
e-mail: ces.org@schwitz.org

Hocamköy

We are a group of people, mainly university students, leading a project called "Hocamköy Eco-village". We want to present ecologically sound alternatives to the many types of human-caused problems and restore the land by creating habitats for native flora and fauna.

In our project, we aim to find practical solutions to immediate ecological problems in Anatolia - solutions developed in co-operation with local peasants and farmers that can serve as a model for other parts of Anatolia. One such problem is large scale migration of villagers, look-

ing for a better life in the cities, where they settle in slums with poor infrastructure. Hocamköy being a self sustaining village will provide an alternative in a form directly relevant to the villagers.

We feel responsible for the biological balance, or rather for restoring the balance disturbed over the centuries. In our efforts we seek to be an integral part of nature. The lands of Central Anatolia have been overexploited over such a long period of time that the barren landscapes can only be restored through a new approach to living as well as production. The Hocamköy experience will lead people to find ways of living naturally and harmoniously.

The main aim of this project is to support and manage the following aspects:

- finding a balanced ecological niche for humans within this ecosystem, tree planting and landscape restoration
- to work towards sustainability, developing social and working contacts with local people
- designing and building ecological houses, using traditional architecture and techniques
- using renewable energy sources, to produce our needs in energy
- recycling organic wastes, on a community level
- organic farming, to meet community needs
- environmental education courses for children, members and the general public to support the establishment of new communities elsewhere
- technical assistance for sustainable developments of villages across Anatolia and collaboration with other eco-villages world-wide.

The project will be one of the first of its kind in Turkey. As a reproducible life model, it will help building an ecocentric future.

Volunteers are welcome, work camps will be arranged.

Contact:
Hocamkoy
Mete Hacaloglu
Kircicegi sok. 5/2
06700 G.O.P. Ankara
Turkey

Tel:
+90 31 24 36 83 78
Fax:
+90 31 24 19 65 92
e-mail:
hocamkoy@metu.edu.tr
web site:
http://hocamkoy.metu.edu.tr

Building in strow-bale at Findhorn Bay, Scotland

Eco-village Networks and Nodes in Europe

Austria:
Peter Lassnig, Gärtnerhof,
Hochwald Str. 37/7, 2230 Gänserndorf
Tel: +43 1 484 73 10

Belguim:
Christine de Wilde, Terre d'Enneille
Grande Enneille 102, 6940 Durbuy
Tel/fax: +32 86 32 34 56
e-mail: terreen@ecovillage.org

Cyprus:
Vincenzo Santiglia, Concordia
101 Tala Square, Tala, Pafos
Tel: +357 665 40 14
Fax: +357 665 40 31
e-mail: vincenzo@cytanet.com.cy

Denmark:
Tomas Sejersen, Landsforeningen for ØkoSamfund, LØS
Egebjergvej 46, 8751 Gedved
Tel: +45 75 66 4111,
Fax: +45 75 66 41 21
e-mail: los@pip.dknet.dk

France:
Marielle Richard (region Parisienne), Reseau Francophone d'Eco-villages
4 allé de Villeneuve l'Etang, 92430 Marnes la Coquette
Tel/Fax: +33 1 47 41 92 34
e-mail: mrichard@atelier.fr

Andrèe Fina, Secrètariat National du Rèseau Francais des Eco-Villages
Bastide „la Source de Vie", Chemin des Riaux, 83570 Carcès
Tel: +33 4 94 04 34 32
web site: www.ecovillages.org/france

Eco-village Networks and Nodes in Europe

Finland:
Marketta Horn, Suomineito-yhteisö
Kaijantie 283, 63700 Ahtari
Tel: +358 65 33 06 01
Fax: +358 65 33 53 23
Mobile: +358 50 584 92 86
e-mail: horn@helsinki.fi

Germany:
Silke Hagmaier, Come Together Netzverk
Ökodorf Sieben Linden 1, 38486 Poppau
Tel: +49 39 00 06 637

Hungary:
Bela Borsos, Gyûrûfu Foundation
Arany Janos utca 16 , 7935 Ibafa,
Tel: +367 335 43 34
e-mail: gyurufu@gyurufu.zpok.hu

Ireland:
Stephan Wik, Eco-Village Network of Ireland
Streamstown, Westport, Co.Mayo
Tel: +353 98 28 417
e-mail: stephan@gaia.org
web site: www.ecovillages.org/ireland

Israel:
Jan Martin Bang, Green Kibbutz
Kibbutz Gezer, 99786 D. N. Shimshon
Tel: +97 28 9 270 650
Fax: +97 28 9 270 736
e-mail: ecowork@mail.gezernet.co.il

Italy:
Barbara Narici, Rete Italiana de Vilaggi Ecologici, RIVE
Via Bertani 2, 20154 Milano
Tel: +39 36 83 01 39 03
Tel/fax: +39 23 15 506

Eco-village Networks and Nodes in Europe

Poland:
Nicole Grospierre, Wiejskie Alternatywne Spolecznosci, W.A.S.
Dabrówka 30, 21-132 Staroscin
Tel: +48 83 65 40 91 ex. 360

Spain:
Richard Wade, Permacultura Montsant
C/Nou 6, 43360 Cornudella de Montsant
Tel: +34 77 82 11 97
e-mail: wade@coac.es

Sweden:
Gunlaug Östbye, NJORD
Carl Westman väg 9, 13335 Salsjöbaden
e-mail: gunlaug@arch.kth.se

Turkey:
Mete Hacaloglu, Eco-Village Network of Turkey
Kircicegi sok. 5/2, 06700 G.O.P. Ankara
Tel: +90 312 436 83 78
Fax: +90 312 446 73 56
e-mail: hocamkoy@marketweb.ner.tr
web site: hocamkoy.metu.edu.tr

United Kingdom:
EVNUK, "B" Bond Warehouse,
Smeaton Road, Bristol, BS1 6XN England
Tel: +44 117 925 05 05
Fax: +44 117 929 72 83
e-mail: evnuk@gaia.org
web site: www.gaia.org/uk

Resource Centres

Folkecentre for Renewable Energy, Denmark

The Folkecentre for Renewable Energy is an independent, non-governmental organisation. It organises courses for individuals or groups from the private sector or from industry. Most of these courses are tailor made although we have an annual programme of workshops and lectures. Examples of courses organised by the Folkecentre:
* Update courses on wind, solar, biogas and co-generation for Danish energy consultants.
* On site training of plumbers on installation of solar heaters.
* Two-weeks course for officials from other countries on wind turbines, water pumping windmills, solar water heaters, biogas, and briquetting, with special emphasis to the application in developing regions and countries.
* Course on wind turbine design, wind farm planning and measurements on wind turbines for engineers.
* One month training of wind energy expert.
* Seminars and conferences on different topics related to renewable energy, environment and sustainable development.

Reports and publications covering our projects are published by FC-Press. The publication list comprises more than 120 titles. Some are available in English although many are only available in Danish.

Contact:
Folkecentre for Renewable Energy
Kammersgaardsvej 16, Sdr. Ydby
7760 Hurup Thy
Denmark

Tel: +45 97 95 66 00
             97 95 65 55
Fax: +45 97 95 65 65
e-mail: Energy@folkecenter.dk
Telex :   7805013 tlxau dk

Mail address: Folkecentre, PO Box 208 , 7760 Hurup Thy, Denmark

Resource Centres

Eurotopia - Leben in Gemeinschaft 1997/98

This is a German language Directory of Communities with addresses and descriptions of 365 European intentional communities.

Please, pay DM 30,- in advance:
Eurocheque made out to Andreas Schaaff Buchversand,
or transfer to Postbank Hamburg,
Bank No. 20010020, Account No. 709 526 205

and order from:
Ökodorf Buchversand,
Dorfstr. 4
29416 Gross-Chüden
Germany

Energy and Environment Centre, Springe, Germany

Practical courses mostly in German on energy saving measures, including rainwater collection, natural sewage systems, water saving devises, solar technology, etc.

Contact:
Energie + Umwelt Zentrum,
31832 Springe-Deister
Germany

Tel.   +49 50 44 975 66
Fax: +49 50 44 975 0

Resource Centres

The Ark Permaculture Project, Clones, Ireland

The Ark Permaculture Project is currently growing into a number of quasi independent resource sharing businesses in the are of developing and installing complete permaculture systems from straw bale, thatch, pole-wood, dwellings to masonry stove, forest gardens, pond and reed bed systems... the current best practice on making sustainability real. The pioneer phase of eventual eco-village development asks that those with immediate practical skills in making things happen go there. Their wish list would also include organic market gardening, engineering, architecture, administration and secretarial work for eco-trade. Courses are also given in permaculture, straw bale construction, reedbed sewage systems, etc.

Contact:
Marcus McCabe, Burdautien, Clones, Co. Monaghan, Ireland

Tel.:   +353 47 52 049
e-mail: arkpc@iol.ie

Centre for Alternative Technology, Wales

Opened in 1975, the Centre for Alternative Technology (C.A.T.) is Europe's leading environmental visitors centre, open every day except Christmas. It promotes and implements sustainable technology, renewable energy, environmental building, alternative sewage systems, energy efficiency, permaculture and organic growing. C.A.T. offers a

large range of practical publications, residential courses, education services and a mail order catalogue of green books and products. Drawing on over 20 years of practical experience it also offers a professional consultancy service which can provide specialist advice and assistance at all levels from initial advice to feasibility studies and project management. C.A.T. is building experimental houses continually and members of staff are living them, making up a small community which is a sort of an eco-village. The centre has helped many starting eco-villages in their early planning, e.g. Cyprus NS has also started an initiative for an Eco-village 2000 in France.

Contact: Charlotte Cosserat
Centre for Alternative Technology
Machynlleth
UK-SY20 9AZ Powys
Wales

Tel.:   +44 16 54 70 24 00
Fax: +44 16 54 70 27 82
e-mail: info@catinfo.demon.co.uk

CENTRE FOR
ALTERNATIVE
TECHNOLOGY

Other GEN Regional Secretariats

GEN-Asia/Oceania
MS 16,
56 Crystal Waters
Qld. 4552,
Australia

Tel: +61 7 54 94 47 41
Fax: +61 7 54 94 45 78
e-mail: lindegger@gen-oceania.org

Eco-village Network of the Americas (ENA)
PO Box 90
Summertown
TN 38483,
USA

Tel: +1 931 96 44 324
Fax: +1 931 96 42 200
e-mail: ecovillage@thefarm.org

GLOBAL
ECO-VILLAGE
NETWORK

The Global Eco-village Network and Europe

Preamble

In 1994 at Fjordvang, Denmark, 20 invited people from 9 eco-villages from all over the world, struck a common note at two consecutive meetings, deciding to network together for the common good. In Spring 1995, in Lebensgarten Steyerberg, Germany, the same group met to consolidate and came up with the idea of going public as the Global Eco-village Network (GEN), that was to invite others in - through the vehicle of a conference to be held at the Findhorn Foundation, Scotland. All those years of quiet personal commitment, with constant celebrations of art, music, nature, people and laughter had an effect on the initiating meetings of GEN. So as well as the dancing and the tree-planting, the meetings and talk were a celebration of commitment - and love. This has been the tenure since.

GEN-Europe

After 480 people from 40 countries gathered for a week to discuss Eco-villages and Sustainable Communities at the Findhorn Foundation, in northern Scotland, the office of the Global Eco-village Network (GEN) for Europe got going in Lebensgarten Steyerberg. The following February, it was already fully into the work of connecting up people and places. At Istanbul on the occasion of the United Nations Habitat II Conference, the Global Eco-village Network was officially inaugurated and elected its first Board. The members are Albert Bates from The Farm. Tennessee, representing the Americas, Max Lindegger for Australia and Oceania including southern Africa, Hamish Stewart from Gaia Villages, as the International Secretariat and holding the connection to our funding organisation Gaia Trust and Prof. Declan Kennedy of Lebensgarten for Europe, Northern Africa and the Middle East.

So what is an *eco-village network* ?

The eco-village movement is new, but it is spreading very quickly in Europe. When the GEN-Europe office was started, there were only eco-village networks in Denmark (LØS), in Germany (IDÖF) and in Israel (an organisation of Green Kibbutzim). That was Spring, 1996. Since then, we have new networks in 6 further countries: Finland had the first meeting in June 1997, as part of the Permaculture Association of that country; France in August; Ireland in October 97; Italy founded

Dyssekilde, Denmark

Grishino, Russia

The Global Eco-village Network and Europe

a network at the meeting in Allesano in Dec. 1996; Russia had an information office in St. Petersburg since 1995, but a network has not been founded so far, although there seems to be 15 to 20 eco-villages or initiatives on the ground. A co-operation with the Sacred Earth Network in Moscow is in progress; Turkey has become a network member in late 1997; and the United Kingdom which has really only one fully fledged eco-village (namely Findhorn Foundation in Scotland), has an organisation called the Eco-Village Network of the United Kingdom (EVNUK) which has been meeting, publishing newsletters and networking since mid-1996.

Many of the members in these networks, particularly in England and France, are people looking for a new way of life, discussing to find their niche, but have not yet made the step to get *an eco-village* going.

We have representatives living in eco-villages and/or starting an information node in 14 other European countries: Gänserndorf near Vienna, Austria; Terre d'Enneille, south of Brussels, Belgium; Latinovac, a peace eco-village in Croatia; Tala near Pafos, Cyprus; Gyürüfü, near Ibafa, as a founding member of GEN in Hungary; Sólheimar - maybe the oldest in Europe (founded 1930) - in Iceland. The Netherlands, Norway, Poland, Portugal, Slovenia and Spain - all have many initiatives, but only one person or planning office acting as information centre - at present; Sweden has a network of long standing: Njörd - that is in the process of deciding whether it wants to be a member of GEN-Europe.

This movement invites us all to say YES to a way of living which addresses the critical issues and enables us to live together with respect for nature. As the eco-village models become established, we can expect to see more and more people moving every year into rural or urban eco-villages or transforming suburbias into eco-villages. We can be witness to eco-village concepts being implemented in cities of Denmark (Fredensgade - Kolding, Torsted-Vest, and Vesterbro, Copenhagen); Germany (Kreuzberg, Berlin and Rehbockstrasse, Hannover) and in the Netherlands (Bikkerhof, Utrecht or Wilhelmina Terrein, Amsterdam). Three of these urban eco-village projects are included in this

Uppachi, Italy

Lakabe, Spain

The Global Eco-village Network and Europe

book. In the GEN-Europe office, we discover new eco-villages or eco-village initiatives almost daily.

Eco-village Self-Audit
GEN is in the process of defining and refining a self-audit tool as part of its work. This will take some time yet and will be circulated when it is finished. In the meantime, Hildur Jackson (GAIA Trust, Denmark) interpreted it as an Eco-village Profile (which is illustrated on page 183) after the GEN mmeting at Findhorn in October 1995. Each of the four elements has four area of concern - that makes 16 areas. You may choose a score between 1 and 4, depending on the degree your project is actually fulfilling the area of concern. The ideal eco-village will thus score 4 times 16 points = 64 points.There was a massive support for this way of defining the common vision, and this is what we understand as "development".

Where do we go from here?
GEN-Europe has applied for registration under the charitable organisation act in Belgium. (It is presently functioning as a members association under the umbrella of the Danish registered Global Eco-village Network.) For the first two years, Christina de Wilde, one of the founding members of the eco-village Terre d'Enneille near Brussels, will be the first President of the Council of GEN-Europe. Declan Ken-nedy will act as Secretary and Agnieszka Komoch as Treasurer. Two further members to the Council will be elected at the first General As-sembly by the members of GEN-Europe, at their meeting in June 1998 in the eco-village Torri Superiore near Ventimiglia, Italy. We hope that the bureaucratic hurdles will have been overcome by then and that GEN-Europe will soon be an NGO of the European Union.

Concluding remarks
The strength of interest in the idea, and the number of projects on the drawing boards is quite startling. From an initial request for informati-on once a week at the beginning of 1996, we have now 15-40 letters, faxes or e-mails per day on an average. What comes out of this information flow is not just beautiful, and well thought out house design with natural materials and vegetable producing gardens, but eco-com-

The Global Eco-village Network and Europe

munitarianism, showing how mediation can create win-win solutions in conflicts among neighbours and at the work-place and how the singing, dancing, hiking and sharing that parallel the continual discussions can help overcome animosities and create friendships - among both old and young. Thank you, everyone.

The urban co-housing in Denmark, Norway and Sweden and the cost-effective ecological settlements in Austria, the Netherlands, Germany, Greece and Switzerland are small contributions in the mainstream to the challenges of creating a sustainable lifestyle in the highly industrialised countries. As the eco-village movement matures, it may help in the ecological re-juvenation of our European cities, towns and suburbs.

Lebensgarten Steyerberg, Germany

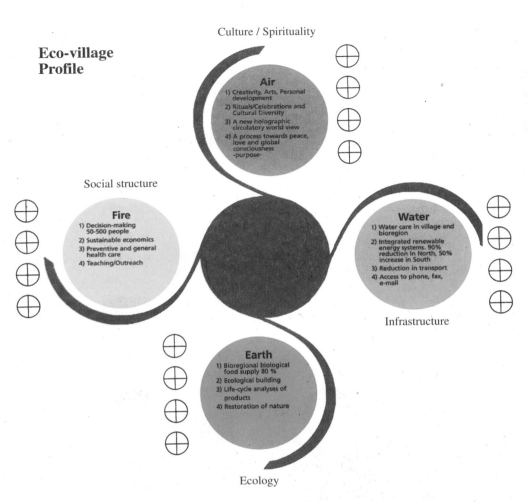

Eco-village Profile

Culture / Spirituality

Air
1) Creativity, Arts, Personal development
2) Rituals/Celebrations and Cultural Diversity
3) A new holographic circulatory world view
4) A process towards peace, love and global consciousness -purpose-

Social structure

Fire
1) Decision-making 50-500 people
2) Sustainable economics
3) Preventive and general health care
4) Teaching/Outreach

Water
1) Water care in village and bioregion
2) Integrated renewable energy systems. 90% reduction in North, 50% increase in South
3) Reduction in transport
4) Access to phone, fax, e-mail

Infrastructure

Earth
1) Bioregional biological food supply 80 %
2) Ecological building
3) Life-cycle analyses of products
4) Restoration of nature

Ecology

Profile user guide

1. Colour 0-4 quarters in the circles above according to the following scheme:

No colour means: No interest in this topic in the eco-village.

One quarter coloured: Interest in the topic, but have done very little.

Two quarters: Quite interested. Have come half way.

Three quarters: Very interested. Almost there - but still room for improvement.

Four quarters: Main area of concern. No room for improvement.

2. Add up your scores. Number of quarters that it is possible to colour ranges from 0-64. Notice where you can still improve. Scores above a certain level, which will have to be agreed upon eg. 48 points and higher would be a qualified eco-village, with at least 2 of points in each element.

**GLOBAL ECO-VILLAGE NETWORK
GEN-EUROPE**

**Ginsterweg 5
D-31595 Steyerberg
Germany
Tel.: + 49 57 64 9 30 40
Fax: + 49 57 64 9 30 42
e-mail: even@lebensgarten.gaia.org
http://www.gaia.org/thegen/geneurope**

Barbro Grindheim, Agnieszka Komoch & Declan Kennedy